MORALS AND DOGMA

Morals And Dogma
Of The
Ancient And
Accepted Scottish Rite

No. 1
Apprentice, Fellow-Craft & Master
(I – III)

MASONICA
Publishers of the Ancient Craft

© 2019 ENTREACACIAS, S.L.

[Publishing House]

Palacio Valdés, 3-5, 1º C
33002 Oviedo - Asturias (Spain)
info@masonica.es
www.masonica.es

First edition: September 2019

MORALS AND DOGMA OF THE ANCIENT AND ACCEPTED SCOTTISH RITE

No. 1
Apprentice, Fellow-Craft & Master
(I – III)

CHARLESTON
A∴ M∴ 5641.

MORALS AND DOGMA

OF

THE ANCIENT AND ACCEPTED SCOTTISH RITE

OF

FREEMASONRY

PREPARED FOR THE

SUPREME COUNCIL OF THE THIRTY-THIRD DEGREE,

FOR THE

SOUTHERN JURISDICTION OF THE UNITED STATES,

AND

PUBLISHED BY ITS AUTHORITY.

CHARLESTON.

A∴ M∴ 5641.

PREFACE.

THE following work has been prepared by authority of the Supreme Council of the Thirty-third Degree, for the Southern [and Western] Jurisdiction of the United States, by the Grand Commander, and is now published by its direction. It contains the Lectures of the Ancient and Accepted Scottish Rite in that jurisdiction, and is specially intended to be read and studied by the Brethren of that obedience, in connection with the Rituals of the Degrees. It is hoped and expected that each will furnish himself with a copy, and make himself familiar with it; for which purpose, as the cost of the work consists entirely in the printing and binding, it will be furnished at a price as moderate as possible. No *individual* will receive pecuniary profit from it, except the agents for its sale.

It has been copyrighted, to prevent its republication elsewhere, and the copyright, like those of all the other works prepared for the Supreme Council, has been assigned to Trustees for that Body. Whatever profits may accrue from it will be devoted to purposes of charity.

The Brethren of the Rite in the United States and Canada *will* be afforded the opportunity to purchase it, nor is it *forbidden* that other Masons shall; but they will not be solicited to do so.

In preparing this work, the Grand Commander has been about equally Author and Compiler; since he has extracted quite half its contents from the works of the best writers and most philosophic or eloquent thinkers. Perhaps it would have been better and more acceptable, if he had extracted more and written less.

Still, perhaps half of it is his own; and, in incorporating here

9

the thoughts and words of others, he has continually changed and added to the language, often intermingling, in the same sentences, his own words with theirs. It not being intended for the world at large, he has felt at liberty to make, from all accessible sources, a Compendium of the Morals and Dogma of the Rite, to re-mould sentences, change and add to words and phrases, com-bine them with his own, and use them as if they were his own, to be dealt with at his pleasure and so availed of as to make the whole most valuable for the purposes intended. He claims, there- fore, little of the merit of authorship, and has not cared to dis- tinguish his own from that which he has taken from other sources, being quite willing that every portion of the book, in turn, may be regarded as borrowed from some old and better writer.

The teachings of these Readings are not sacramental, so far as they go beyond the realm of Morality into those of other domains of Thought and Truth. The Ancient aud Accepted Scottish Rite uses the word "Dogma" in its true sense, of *doctrine*, or *teaching ;* and is not *dogmatic* in the odious sense of that term. Every one is entirely free to reject and dissent from whatsoever herein may seem to him to be untrue or unsound. It is only required of him ₋hat he shall weigh what is taught, and give it fair hearing and unprejudiced judgment. Of course, the ancient theosophic and philosophic speculations are not embodied as part of the *doctrines* of the Rite ; but because it is of interest and profit to know what the Ancient Intellect thought upon these subjects, and because nothing so conclusively proves the radical difference between our human and the animal nature, as the capacity of the human mind to entertain such speculations in regard to itself and the Deity. But as to these opinions themselves, we may say, in the words of the learned Canonist, Ludovicus Gomez: *" Opiniones secumdum varietatem tempurumo senescat et intermoriantur, alioque diversas vel proribus contrario renascantur et dennde pubescant"*

MORALS AND DOGMA.

L

APPRENTICE.

THE TWELVE-INCH RULE AND COMMON GAVEL.

FORCE, unregulated or ill-regulated, is not only wasted in the void, like that of gunpowder burned in the open air, and steam unconfined by science; but, striking in the dark, and its blows meeting only the air, they recoil, and bruise itself. It is destruction and ruin. It is the volcano, the earthquake, the cyclone;—not growth and progress. It is Polyphemus blinded, striking at random, and falling headlong among the sharp rocks by the impetus of his own blows.

The blind Force of the people is a Force that must be econ—omized, and also managed, as the blind Force of steam, lifting the ponderous iron arms and turning the large wheels, is made to bore and rifle the cannon and to weave the most delicate lace. It must be regulated by Intellect. Intellect is to the people and the people's Force, what the slender needle of the compass is to the ship—its soul, always counselling the huge mass of wood and iron, and always pointing to the north. To attack the citadels built up on all sides against the human race by superstitions, despotisms, and prejudices, the Force must have a brain and a law. Then its leads of daring produce permanent results, and there is real progress. Then there are sublime conquests. Thought is a force, and philosophy should be an energy, finding its aim and its effects in the amelioration of mankind. The two great motors are Truth and Love. When all these Forces are combined, and guided by the Intellect, and regulated by the RULE of Right, and Justice, and of combined and systematic movement and effort, the great revolution prepared for by the ages will begin to march. The POWER of the Deity Himself is in equilibrium with His WISDOM. Hence only results HARMONY.

It is because Force is illy regulated, that revolutions prove failures. Therefore it is that so often insurrections, coming from those high mountains that domineer over the moral horizon, Justice, Wisdom, Reason, Right, built of the purest snow of the ideal, after a long fall from rock to rock, after having reflected the sky in their transparency, and been swollen by a hundred affluents, in the majestic path of triumph, suddenly lose themselves in quagmires, like a Californian river in the sands.

The onward march of the human race requires that the heights around it should blaze with noble and enduring lessons of courage. Deeds of daring dazzle history, and form one class of the guiding lights of man. They are the stars and coruscations from that great sea of electricity, the Force inherent in the people. To strive, to brave all risks, to perish, to persevere, to be true to one's self, to grapple body to body with destiny, to surprise defeat by the little terror it inspires, now to confront unrighteous power, now to defy intoxicated triumph—these are the examples that the nations need, and the light that electrifies them.

There are immense Forces in the great caverns of evil beneath society; in the hideous degradation, squalor, wretchedness and destitution, vices and crimes that reek and simmer in the darkness in that populace below the people, of great cities. There disinter-estedness vanishes, every one howls, searches, gropes, and gnaws for himself. Ideas are ignored, and of progress there is no thought. This populace has two mothers, both of them step-mothers—Ignorance and Misery. Want is their only guide—for the appetite alone they crave satisfaction.

Yet even these may be employed. The lowly sand we trample upon, cast into the furnace, melted, purified *by* fire, may become resplendent crystal. They have the brute force of the HAMMER, but their blows help on the great cause, when struck within the lines traced by the RULE held by wisdom and discretion.

Yet it is this very Force of the people, this Titanic power of the giants, that builds the fortifications of tyrants, and is embodied in their armies. Hence the possibility of such tyrannies as those of which it has been said, that "Rome smells worse under Vitellius than under Sylla. Under Claudius and under Domitian there is a deformity of baseness corresponding to the ugliness of the tyranny. The foulness of the slaves is a direct result of the atrocious baseness of the despot. A miasma exhales from these crouching consciences that reflect the master; the public authorities are unclean, hearts are collapsed, consciences shrunken, souls puny. This is so under Caracalla, it is so under Commodus, it is so under Heliogabalus, while from the Roman senate, under Cæsar, there comes only the rank odor peculiar to the eagle's eyrie."

It is the force of the people that sustains all these despotisms, the basest as well as the best. That force acts through armies; and these oftener enslave than liberate. Despotism there applies the RULE. Force is the MACE of steel at the saddle-bow of the knight or of the bishop in armor. Passive obedience by force supports thrones and oligarchies, Spanish kings, and Venetian senates Might, in an army wielded by tyranny, is the enormous sum total of utter weakness; and so Humanity wages war against Humanity, in despite of Humanity. So a people willingly submits to despotism, and its workmen submit to be despised, and its soldiers to be whipped; therefore it is that battles lost by a nation are often progress attained. Less glory is more liberty. When the drum is silent, reason sometimes speaks.

Tyrants use the force of the people to chain and subjugate—that is, enyoke the people. Then they plough with them as men do with oxen yoked. Thus the spirit of liberty and innovation is reduced by bayonets, and principles are struck dumb by cannon-shot; while the monks mingle with the troopers, and the Church militant and jubilant, Catholic or Puritan, sings Te Deums for victories over rebellion.

The military power, not subordinate to the civil power, again the HAMMER or MACE of FORCE, independent of the RULE, is an armed tyranny, born full-grown, as Athené sprung from the brain of Zeus. It spawns a dynasty, and begins with Cæsar to rot into

Vitellius and Commodus. At the present day it inclines to *begin* where former dynasties *ended.*

Constantly the people put forth immense strength, only to end in immense weakness. The force of the people is exhausted in indefinitely prolonging things long since dead; in governing mankind by embalming old dead tyrannies of Faith; restoring dilapidated dogmas; regilding faded, worm-eaten shrines; whitening and rouging ancient and barren superstitions; saving society by multiplying parasites; perpetuating superannuated institutions; enforcing the worship of symbols as the actual means of salvation; and tying the dead corpse of the Past, mouth to mouth, with the living Present. Therefore it is that it is one of the fatalities of Humanity to be condemned to eternal struggles with phantoms, with superstitions, bigotries, hypocrisies, prejudices, the formulas of error, and the pleas of tyranny. Despotisms, seen in the past, become respectable, as the mountain, bristling with volcanic rock, rugged and horrid, seen through the haze of distance is blue and smooth and beautiful. The sight of a single dungeon of tyranny is worth more, to dispel illusions, and create a holy hatred of despotism, and to direct FORCE aright, than the most eloquent volumes. The French should have preserved the Bastile as a perpetual lesson; Italy should not destroy the dungeons of the Inquisition. The Force of the people maintained the Power that built its gloomy cells, and placed the living in their granite sepulchres.

The FORCE of the people cannot, by its unrestrained and fitful action, maintain and continue in action and existence a free Government once created. That Force must be limited, restrained, conveyed by distribution into different channels, and by roundabout courses, to outlets, whence it is to issue as the law, action, and decision of the State; as the wise old Egyptian kings conveyed in different canals, by sub-division, the swelling waters of the Nile, and compelled them to fertilize and not devastate the land. There must be the *jus et norma*, the law and *Rule*, or *Gauge*, of constitution and law, within which the public force must act. Make a breach in either, and the great steam-hammer, with its swift and ponderous blows, crushes all the machinery to atoms, and, at last, wrenching itself away, lies inert and dead amid the ruin it has wrought.

The FORCE of the people, or the popular will, in action and

exerted, symbolized by the GAVEL, regulated and guided by and acting within the limits of LAW and ORDER, symbolized by the TWENTY-FOUR-INCH RULE, has for its fruit LIBERTY, EQUALITY, and FRATERNITY,—liberty regulated by law; equality of rights in the eye of the law; brotherhood with its duties and obligations as well as its benefits.

You will hear shortly of the *Rough* ASHLAR and the *Perfect* ASHLAR, as part of the jewels of the Lodge. The rough Ashlar is said to be "a stone, as taken from the quarry, in its rude and natural state." The perfect Ashlar is said to be "a stone made ready by the hands of the workmen, to bé adjusted by the working-tools of the Fellow-Craft." We shall not repeat the explanations of these symbols given by the York Rite. You may read them in its printed monitors. They are declared to allude to the self-improvement of the individual craftsman,—a continuation of the same superficial interpretation.

The rough Ashlar is the PEOPLE, as a mass, rude and unorganized. The perfect Ashlar, or cubical stone, symbol of perfection, is the STATE, the rulers deriving their powers from the consent of the governed; the constitution and laws speaking the will of the people; the government harmonious, symmetrical, efficient,—its powers properly distributed and duly adjusted in equilibrium.

If we delineate a cube on a plane surface thus:

we have visible *three* faces, and *nine* external lines, drawn between *seven* points. The complete cube has *three* more faces, making *six; three* more lines, making *twelve;* and *one* more point, making *eight.* As the number 12 includes the sacred numbers 3, 5, 7, and 3 times 3, or 9, and is produced by adding the sacred number 3 to 9; while its own two figures, 1, 2, the unit or monad, and duad, added together, make the same sacred number 3; it was called the perfect number; and the cube became the symbol of perfection.

Produced by FORCE, acting by RULE; hammered in accordance

w.th lines measured by the Gauge, out of the rough Ashlar, it is
an appropriate symbol of the Force of the people, expressed as the
constitution and law of the State; and of the State itself the three
visible faces represent the three departments,—the Executive,
which executes the laws; the Legislative, which makes the laws;
the Judiciary, which interprets the laws, applies and enforces
them, between man and man, between the State and the citizens.
The three invisible faces, are Liberty, Equality, and Fraternity,—
the threefold soul of the State—its vitality, spirit, and intellect.

*　　　*　　　*　　　*　　　*　　　*

Though Masonry neither usurps the place of, nor apes religion,
prayer is an essential part of our ceremonies. It is the aspiration
of the soul toward the Absolute and Infinite Intelligence, which
is the One Supreme Deity, most feebly and misunderstandingly
characterized as an "ARCHITECT." Certain faculties of man are
directed toward the Unknown — thought, meditation, prayer.
The unknown is an ocean, of which conscience is the compass.
Tnought, meditation, prayer, are the great mysterious pointings
of the needle. It is a spiritual magnetism that thus connects the
human soul with the Deity. These majestic irradiations of the soul
pierce through the shadow toward the light.

It is but a shallow scoff to say that prayer is absurd, because
it is not possible for us, by means of it, to persuade God to change
His plans. He produces foreknown and foreintended effects, by
the instrumentality of the forces of nature, all of which are
His forces. Our own are part of these. Our free agency and
our will are forces. We do not absurdly cease to make *efforts* to
attain wealth or happiness, prolong life, and continue health,
because we cannot by any effort change what is predestined. If
the effort also is predestined, it is not the less *our* effort, made of
our free will. So, likewise, we pray. Will is a force. Thought is
a force. Prayer is a force. Why should it not be of the law of
God, that prayer, like Faith and Love, should have its effects? Man
's not to be comprehended as a starting-point, or progress as a goal,
without those two great forces, Faith and Love. Prayer is sublime.
Orisons that beg and clamor are pitiful. To deny the efficacy of
prayer, is to deny that of Faith, Love, and Effort. Yet the effects
produced, when our hand, moved by our will, launches a pebble
into the ocean, never cease; and every uttered word is registered
for eternity upon the invisible air.

Every Lodge is a Temple, and as a whole, and in its details, symbolic. The universe itself supplied man with the model for the first temples reared to the Divinity. The arrangement of the Temple of Solomon, the symbolic ornaments which formed its chief decorations, and the dress of the High-Priest, all had reference to the order of the universe, as then understood. The Temple contained many emblems of the seasons—the sun, the moon, the planets, the constellations Ursa Major and Minor, the zodiac, the elements, and the other parts of the world. It is the Master of *this* Lodge, of the Universe, Hermes, of whom Khirom is the representative, that is one of the lights of the Lodge.

For further instruction as to the symbolism of the heavenly bodies, and of the sacred numbers, and of the temple and its details, you must wait patiently until you advance in Masonry, in the mean time exercising your intellect in studying them for yourself. To study and seek to interpret correctly the symbols of the universe, is the work of the sage and philosopher. It is to decipher the writing of God, and penetrate into His thoughts.

This is what is asked and answered in our catechism, in regard to the Lodge.

*   *   *   *   *   *

A "Lodge" is defined to be "an assemblage of Freemasons, duly congregated, having the sacred writings, square, and compass, and a charter, or warrant of constitution, authorizing them to work." The room or place in which they meet, representing some part of King Solomon's Temple, is also called the Lodge; and it is that we are now considering.

It is said to be supported by three great columns, WISDOM, FORCE or STRENGTH, and BEAUTY, represented by the Master, the Senior Warden, and the Junior Warden; and these are said to be the columns that support the Lodge, "because Wisdom, Strength, and Beauty, are the perfections of everything, and nothing can endure without them." "Because," the York Rite says, "it is necessary that there should be Wisdom to conceive, Strength to support, and Beauty to adorn, all great and important undertakings." "Know ye not," says the Apostle Paul, "that ye are the temple of God, and that the spirit of God dwelleth in you? If any man desecrate the temple of God, him shall God destroy, for the temple of God is holy, which temple ye are."

The Wisdom and Power of the Deity are in equilibrium. The

laws of nature and the moral laws are not the mere despotic man-
dates of His Omnipotent will; for, then they might be changed by
H.m, and order become disorder, and good and right become evil
and wrong; honesty and loyalty, vices; and fraud, ingratitude, and
vice, virtues. Omnipotent power, infinite, and existing alone,
would necessarily not be constrained to consistency. Its decrees
and laws could not be immutable. The laws of God are not obligatory on us, because they are the enactments of His POWER, or
the expression of His WILL; but because they express His infinite
WISDOM. They are not right because they are His laws, but His
laws because they are right. From the equilibrium of infinite
wisdom and infinite force, results perfect harmony, in physics and
in the moral universe. Wisdom, Power, and Harmony constitute
one Masonic triad. They have other and profounder meanings,
that may at some time be unveiled to you.

As to the ordinary and commonplace explanation, it may be
added, that the wisdom of the Architect is displayed in combining,
as only a skillful Architect can do, and as God has done everywhere,—for example, in the tree, the human frame, the egg, the
cells of the honeycomb—strength, with grace, beauty, symmetry,
proportion, lightness, ornamentation. That, too, is the perfection of the orator and poet—to combine force, strength, energy,
with grace of style, musical cadences, the beauty of figures, the
play and irradiation of imagination and fancy; and so, in a
State, the warlike and industrial force of the people, and their
Titanic strength, must be combined with the beauty of the
arts, the sciences, and the intellect, if the State would scale
the heights of excellence, and the people be really free. Harmony in this, as in all the Divine, the material, and the
human, is the result of equilibrium, of the sympathy and opposite
action of contraries; a single Wisdom above them holding the
beam of the scales. To reconcile the moral law, human responsi-
bility, free-will, with the absolute power of God; and the existence
of evil with His absolute wisdom, and goodness, and mercy,—these
are the great enigmas of the Sphynx.

You entered the Lodge between two columns. They represent
the two which stood in the porch of the Temple, on each side of
the great eastern gateway. These pillars, of bronze, four fingers
breadth in thickness, were, according to the most authentic

account—that in the First and that in the Second Book of Kings, confirmed in Jeremiah—eighteen cubits high, with a capital five cubits high. The shaft of each was four cubits in diameter. A cubit is one foot and $\frac{181}{365}$. That is, the shaft of each was a little over thirty feet eight inches in height, the capital of each a little over eight feet six inches in height, and the diameter of the shaft six feet ten inches. The capitals were enriched by pomegranates of bronze, covered by bronze net-work, and ornamented with wreaths of bronze; and appear to have imitated the shape of the seed-vessel of the lotus or Egyptian lily, a sacred symbol to the Hindus and Egyptians. The pillar or column on the right, or in the south, was named, as the Hebrew word is rendered in our translation of the Bible, JACHIN: and that on the left BOAZ. Our translators say that the first word means, "*He shall establish;*" and the second, "*In it is strength.*"

These columns were imitations, by Khûrûm, the Tyrian artist, of the great columns consecrated to the Winds and Fire, at the entrance to the famous Temple of Malkarth, in the city of Tyre. It is customary, in Lodges of the York Rite, to see a celestial globe on one, and a terrestrial globe on the other; but these are not warranted, if the object be to imitate the original two columns of the Temple. The symbolic meaning of these columns we shall leave for the present unexplained, only adding that Entered Apprentices keep their working-tools in the column JACHIN; and giving you the etymology and literal meaning of the two names.

The word *Jachin*, in Hebrew, is יכין. It was probably pronounced *Ya-kayan*, and meant, as a verbal noun, *He that strengthens*; and thence, *firm, stable, upright.*

The word *Boaz* is בעז, Baaz. עז means *Strong, Strength, Power, Might, Refuge, Source of Strength, a Fort.* The ב prefixed means "*with*" or "*in*," and gives the word the force of the Latin gerund, *roborando—Strengthening.*

The former word also means *he will establish*, or *plant in an erect position*—from the verb כן *Kûn, he stood erect.* It probably meant *Active* and *Vivifying Energy* and *Force;* and *Boaz, Stability, Permanence*, in the *passive* sense.

The Dimensions of the Lodge, our Brethren of the York Rite say, " are unlimited, and its covering no less than the canopy of heaven." " To this object," they say, " the mason's mind is con

tinually directed, and thither he hopes at last to arrive by the
aid of the theological ladder which Jacob in his vision saw
ascending from earth to heaven; the three principal rounds of
which are denominated Faith, Hope, and Charity; and which
admonish us to have Faith in God, Hope in Immortality, and
Charity to all mankind." Accordingly a ladder, sometimes with
nine rounds, is seen on the chart, resting at the bottom on the
earth, its top in the clouds, the stars shining above it; and this is
deemed to represent that mystic ladder, which Jacob saw in his
dream, set up on the earth, and the top of it reaching to heaven,
with the angels of God ascending and descending on it. The
addition of the three principal rounds to the symbolism, is wholly
modern and incongruous.

The ancients counted seven planets, thus arranged: the Moon,
Mercury, Venus, the Sun, Mars, Jupiter, and Saturn. There
were seven heavens and seven spheres of these planets; on all
the monuments of Mithras are seven altars or pyres, consecrated
to the seven planets, as were the seven lamps of the golden
candelabrum in the Temple. That these represented the planets,
we are assured by Clemens of Alexandria, in his Stromata, and by
Philo Judæus.

To return to its source in the Infinite, the human soul, the
ancients held, had to ascend, as it had descended, through the
seven spheres. The *Ladder* by which it reascends, has, according
to Marsilius Ficinus, in his Commentary on the Ennead of Plo-
tinus, seven degrees or steps; and in the mysteries of Mithras,
carried to Rome under the Emperors, the ladder, with its seven
rounds, was a symbol referring to this ascent through the spheres
of the seven planets. Jacob saw the Spirits of God ascending and
descending on it; and above it the Deity Himself. The Mithriac
mysteries were celebrated in caves, where gates were marked at
the four equinoctial and solstitial points of the zodiac; and the
seven planetary spheres were represented, which souls needs must
traverse in descending from the heaven of the fixed stars to the
elements that envelop the earth; and seven gates were marked,
one for each planet, through which they pass, in descending or
returning.

We learn this from Celsus, in Origen, who says that the symbolic image of this passage among the stars, used in the Mithriac
mysteries, was a ladder reaching from earth to heaven, divided

into seven steps or stages, to each of which was a gate, and at the summit an eighth one, that of the fixed stars. The symbol was the same as that of the seven stages of Borsippa, the Pyramid of vitrified brick, near Babylon, built of seven stages, and each of a different color. In the Mithriac ceremonies, the candidate went through seven stages of initiation, passing through many fearful trials—and of these the high ladder with seven rounds or steps was the symbol.

You see the Lodge, its details and ornaments, by its Lights. You have already heard what these Lights, the greater and lesser, are said to be, and how they are spoken of by our Brethren of the York Rite.

The *Holy Bible, Square, and Compass*, are not only styled the Great Lights in Masonry, but they are also technically called the *Furniture* of the Lodge; and, as you have seen, it is held that there is no Lodge without them. This has sometimes been made a pretext for excluding Jews from our Lodges, because they cannot regard the New Testament as a holy book. The Bible is an indispensable part of the furniture of a *Christian* Lodge, only because it is the sacred book of the Christian religion. The Hebrew Pentateuch in a Hebrew Lodge, and the Koran in a Mohammedan one, belong on the Altar; and one of these, and the Square and Compass, properly understood, are the Great Lights by which a Mason must walk and work.

The obligation of the candidate is always to be taken on the sacred book or books of his religion, that he may deem it more solemn and binding; and therefore it was that you were asked of what religion you were. We have no other concern with your religious creed.

The Square is a right angle, formed by two right lines. It is adapted only to a plane surface, and belongs only to geometry, earth-measurement, that trigonometry which deals only with planes, and with the earth, which the ancients supposed to be a plane. The Compass describes circles, and deals with spherical trigonometry, the science of the spheres and heavens. The former, therefore, is an emblem of what concerns the earth and the body; the latter of what concerns the heavens and the soul. Yet the Compass is also used in plane trigonometry, as in erecting perpendiculars; and, therefore, you are reminded that, although in this degree both points of the Compass are under the Square, and

you are now dealing only with the moral and political meaning of
the symbols, and not with their philosophical and spiritual meanings, still the divine ever mingles with the human; with the
earthly the spiritual intermixes; and there is something spiritual
in the commonest duties of life. The nations are not bodies-
politic alone, but also souls-politic; and woe to that people which,
seeking the material only, forgets that it has a soul. Then we
have a race, petrified in dogma, which presupposes the absence of
a soul and the presence only of memory and instinct, or demoral-
ized by lucre. Such a nature can never lead civilization. Genu-
flexion before the idol or the dollar atrophies the muscle which
walks and the will which moves. Hieratic or mercantile absorption diminishes the radiance of a people, lowers its horizon by
lowering its level, and deprives it of that understanding of the
universal aim, at the same time human and divine, which makes
the missionary nations. A free people, forgetting that it has a soul
to be cared for, devotes all its energies to its material advancement.
If it makes war, it is to subserve its commercial interests. The
citizens copy after the State, and regard wealth, pomp, and luxury
as the great goods of life. Such a nation creates wealth rapidly,
and distributes it badly. Thence the two extremes, of monstrous
opulence and monstrous misery; all the enjoyment to a few, all
the privations to the rest, that is to say, to the people; Privilege,
Exception, Monopoly, Feudality, springing up from Labor itself:
a false and dangerous situation, which, making Labor a blinded
and chained Cyclops, in the mine, at the forge, in the workshop, at
the loom, in the field, over poisonous fumes, in miasmatic cells, in
unventilated factories, founds public power upon private misery,
and plants the greatness of the State in the suffering of the individual. It is a greatness illy constituted, in which all the material
elements are combined, and into which no moral element enters.
If a people, like a star, has the right of eclipse, the light ought to
return. The eclipse should not degenerate into night.

The three lesser, or the Sublime Lights, you have heard, are the
Sun, the Moon, and the Master of the Lodge; and you have heard
what our Brethren of the York Rite say in regard to them, and
why they hold them to be Lights of the Lodge. But the Sun and
Moon do in no sense light the Lodge, unless it be symbolically,
and then the lights are not they, but those things of which they
are the symbols. Of what they are the symbols the Mason in that

Rite is not told. Nor does the Moon in any sense rule the night with regularity. The Sun is the ancient symbol of the life-giving and generative power of the Deity. To the ancients, light was the cause of life; and God was the source from which all light flowed; the *essence* of Light, the *Invisible* Fire, developed as Flame *manifested* as light and splendor. The Sun was his manifestation and visible image; and the Sabæans worshipping the Light—God, *seemed* to worship the Sun, in whom they saw the manifestation of the Deity.

The Moon was the symbol of the passive capacity of nature to produce, the female, of which the life-giving power and energy was the male. It was the symbol of Isis, Astarte, and Artemis, or Diana. The "*Master of Life*" was the Supreme Deity, above both, and manifested through both ; Zeus, the Son of Saturn, become King of the Gods ; Horus, son of Osiris and Isis, become the Master of Life; Dionusos or Bacchus, like Mithras, become the author of Light and Life and Truth.

    *   *   *   *   *   *

The Master of Light and Life, the Sun and the Moon, are symbolized in every Lodge by the Master and Wardens: and this makes it the duty of the Master to dispense light to the Brethren, by himself, and through the Wardens, who are his ministers.

"Thy sun," says ISAIAH to Jerusalem, "shall no more go down, neither shall thy moon withdraw itself; for the LORD shall be thine everlasting light, and the days of thy mourning shall be ended. Thy people also shall be all righteous; they shall inherit the land forever." Such is the type of a free people.

Our northern ancestors worshipped this tri-une Deity; ODIN, the Almighty FATHER; FREA, his wife, emblem of universal matter and THOR, his son, the mediator. But above all these was the Supreme God, "the author of everything that existeth, the Eternal, the Ancient, the Living and Awful Being, the Searcher into concealed things, the Being that never changeth." In the Temple of Eleusis (a sanctuary lighted only by a window in the roof, and representing the universe), the images of the Sun, Moon, and Mercury, were represented.

"The Sun and Moon," says the learned Bro∴ DELAULNAYE, "represent the two grand principles of all generations, the active and passive, the male and the female. The Sun represents the actual Light. He pours upon the Moon his fecundating rays; both shed their light upon their offspring, the Blazing Star, or HORUS, and the three form the great Equilateral Triangle, in the centre of which is the omnific letter of the Kabalah, by which creation is said to have been effected."

The ORNAMENTS of a Lodge are said to be "the Mosaic Pavement, the Indented Tessel, and the Blazing Star." The Mosaic Pavement, chequered in squares or lozenges, is said to represent the ground-floor of King Solomon's Temple; and the Indented Tessel "that beautiful tesselated border which surrounded it." The Blazing Star in the centre is said to be "an emblem of Divine Providence, and commemorative of the star which appeared to guide the wise men of the East to the place of our Saviour's nativity." But "there was no stone seen" within the Temple. The walls were covered with planks of cedar, and the floor was covered with planks of fir. There is no evidence that there was such a pavement or floor in the Temple, or such a bordering. In England, anciently, the Tracing-Board was surrounded with an indented border; and it is only in America that such a border is put around the Mosaic pavement. The tesseræ, indeed, are the squares or lozenges of the pavement. In England, also, "the indented or denticulated border" is called "tesselated," because it has four "tassels," said to represent Temperance, Fortitude, Prudence, and Justice. It was termed the Indented Trassel; but this is a misuse of words. It is a *tesserated* pavement, with an indented border round it.

The pavement, alternately black and white, symbolizes, whether so intended or not, the Good and Evil Principles of the Egyptian and Persian creed. It is the warfare of Michael and Satan, of the Gods and Titans, of Balder and Lok; between light and shadow, which is darkness; Day and Night; Freedom and Despotism; Religious Liberty and the Arbitrary Dogmas of a Church that thinks for its votaries, and whose Pontiff claims to be infallible, and the decretals of its Councils to constitute a gospel.

The edges of this pavement, if in lozenges, will necessarily be indented or denticulated, toothed like a saw; and to complete and finish it a bordering is necessary. It is completed by tassels as ornaments at the corners. If these and the bordering have any symbolic meaning, it is fanciful and arbitrary.

To find in the BLAZING STAR of five points an allusion to the

Divine Providence, is also fanciful; and to make it commemorative of the Star that is said to have guided the Magi, is to give it a meaning comparatively modern. Originally it represented SIRIUS, or the Dog-star, the forerunner of the inundation of the Nile; the God ANUBIS, companion of ISIS in her search for the body of OSIRIS, her brother and husband. Then it became the image of HORUS, the son of OSIRIS, himself symbolized also by the Sun, the author of the Seasons, and the God of Time; Son of ISIS, who was the universal nature, himself the primitive matter, inexhaustible source of Life, spark of uncreated fire, universal seed of all beings. It was HERMES, also, the Master of Learning, whose name in Greek is that of the God Mercury. It became the sacred and potent sign or character of the Magi, the PENTALPHA, and is the significant emblem of Liberty and Freedom, blazing with a steady radiance amid the weltering elements of good and evil of Revolutions, and promising serene skies and fertile seasons to the nations, after the storms of change and tumult.

In the East of the Lodge, over the Master, inclosed in a triangle, is the Hebrew letter YŌD [י or *aī*]. In the English and American Lodges the Letter G.·. is substituted for this, as the initial of the word GOD, with as little reason as if the letter D., initial of DIEU, were used in French Lodges instead of the proper letter. YŌD is, in the Kabalah, the symbol of Unity, of the Supreme Deity, the first letter of the Holy Name; and also a symbol of the Great Kabalistic Triads. To understand its mystic meanings, you must open the pages of the Sohar and Siphra de Zeniutha, and other kabalistic books, and ponder deeply on their meaning. It must suffice to say, that it is the Creative Energy of the Deity, is represented as a *point*, and that point in the centre of the *Circle* of immensity. It is to us in this degree, the symbol of that unmanifested Deity, the Absolute, who has no name.

Our French Brethren place this letter YŌD in the centre of the Blazing Star. And in the old Lectures, our ancient English Brethren said, "The Blazing Star or Glory in the centre refers us to that grand luminary, the Sun, which enlightens the earth, and by its genial influence dispenses blessings to mankind." They called it also in the same lectures, an emblem of PRUDENCE. The word *Prudentia* means, in its original and fullest signification, *Foresight;* and, accordingly, the Blazing Star has been regarded as an emblem of Omniscience, or the All-seeing Eye, which to the

2

Egyptian Initiates was the emblem of Osiris, the Creator. With
the YŌD in the centre, it has the kabalistic meaning of the Divine
Energy, manifested as Light, creating the universe.

The Jewels of the Lodge are said to be six in number. Three
are called " *Movable*," and three " *Immovable*." The SQUARE, the
LEVEL, and the PLUMB were anciently and properly called the
Movable Jewels, because they pass from one Brother to another.
It is a modern innovation to call them immovable, because they
must always be present in the Lodge. The immovable jewels are
the ROUGH ASHLAR, the PERFECT ASHLAR or CUBICAL STONE, or,
in some Rituals, the DOUBLE CUBE, and the TRACING-BOARD, or
TRESTLE-BOARD.

Of these jewels our Brethren of the York Rite say: " The
Square inculcates Morality; the *Level*, Equality; and the *Plumb*,
Rectitude of Conduct." Their explanation of the immovable
jewels may be read in their monitors.

     *   *   *   *   *   *

Our Brethren of the York Rite say that "there is represented
in every well-governed Lodge, a certain point, within a circle;
the point representing an individual Brother; the Circle, the
boundary line of his conduct, beyond which he is never to suffer
his prejudices or passions to betray him."

This is not to *interpret* the symbols of Masonry. It is said by
some, with a nearer approach to interpretation, that the point
within the circle represents God in the centre of the universe. It
is a common Egyptian sign for the Sun and Osiris, and is still
used as the astronomical sign of the great luminary. In the Kabalah the point is YŌD, the Creative Energy of God, irradiating
with light the circular space which God, the universal Light,
left vacant, wherein to create the worlds, by withdrawing his
substance of Light back on all sides from one point.

Our Brethren add that, "this circle is embordered by two
perpendicular parallel lines, representing Saint John the Baptist
and Saint John the Evangelist, and upon the top rest the Holy
Scriptures" (an open book). " In going round this circle," they
say, " we necessarily touch upon these two lines as well as upon
the Holy Scriptures; and while a Mason keeps himself circum-
scribed within their precepts, it is impossible that he should
materially err."

30

It would be a waste of time to comment upon this. Some writers have imagined that the parallel lines represent the Tropics of Cancer and Capricorn, which the Sun alternately touches upon at the summer and winter solstices. But the tropics are not perpendicular lines, and the idea is merely fanciful. If the parallel lines ever belonged to the ancient symbol, they had some more recondite and more *fruitful* meaning. They probably had the same meaning as the twin columns Jachin and Boaz. That meaning is not for the Apprentice. The adept may find it in the Kabalah. The JUSTICE and MERCY of God are in equilibrium, and the result is HARMONY, because a Single and Perfect Wisdom presides over both.

The Holy Scriptures are an entirely modern addition to the symbol, like the terrestrial and celestial globes on the columns of the portico. Thus the ancient symbol has been denaturalized by incongruous additions, like that of Isis weeping over the broken column containing the remains of Osiris at Byblos.

* * * * * *

Masonry has its decalogue, which is a law to its Initiates. These are its Ten Commandments:

I. ⊕∴ God is the Eternal, Omnipotent, Immutable WISDOM and Supreme INTELLIGENCE and Exhaustless LOVE.

Thou shalt adore, revere, and love Him!

Thou shalt honor Him by practising the virtues!

II. ○∴ Thy religion shall be, to do good because it is a pleasure to thee, and not merely because it is a duty.

That thou mayest become the friend of the wise man, thou shalt obey his precepts!

Thy soul is immortal! Thou shalt do nothing to degrade it!

III. ⊕∴ Thou shalt unceasingly war against vice!

Thou shalt not do unto others that which thou wouldst not wish them to do unto thee!

Thou shalt be submissive to thy fortunes, and keep burning the light of wisdom!

IV. ○∴ Thou shalt honor thy parents!

Thou shalt pay respect and homage to the aged!

Thou shalt instruct the young!

Thou shalt protect and defend infancy and innocence!

V. ⊕∴ Thou shalt cherish thy wife and thy children!

Thou shalt love thy country, and obey its laws!

VI. O∴ Thy friend shall be to thee a second self!
Misfortune shall not estrange thee from him!
Thou shalt do for his memory whatever thou wouldst do for
him, if he were living!

VII. ⊕∴ Thou shalt avoid and flee from insincere friendships!
Thou shalt in everything refrain from excess!
Thou shalt fear to be the cause of a stain on thy memory.

VIII. O∴ Thou shalt allow no passion to become thy master!
Thou shalt make the passions of others profitable lessons to
thyself.
Thou shalt be indulgent to error!

IX. ⊕∴ Thou shalt hear much: Thou shalt speak little: Thou
shalt act well!
Thou shalt forget injuries!
Thou shalt render good for evil!
Thou shalt not misuse either thy strength or thy superiority!

X. O∴ Thou shalt study to know men; that thereby thou may-
est learn to know thyself!
Thou shalt ever seek after virtue!
Thou shalt be just!
Thou shalt avoid idleness!

But the great commandment of Masonry is this: "A new commandment give I unto you: that ye love one another! He that
saith he is in the light, and hateth his brother, remaineth still in
the darkness."

Such are the moral duties of a Mason. But it is also the duty
of Masonry to assist in elevating the moral and intellectual level
of society; in coining knowledge, bringing ideas into circulation,
and causing the mind of youth to grow; and in putting, gradually,
by the teachings of axioms and the promulgation of positive laws,
the human race in harmony with its destinies.

To this duty and work the Initiate is apprenticed. He must not
imagine that he can effect nothing, and, therefore, despairing, become inert. It is in this, as in a man's daily life. Many great
deeds are done in the small struggles of life. There is, we are told,
a determined though unseen bravery, which defends itself, foot to
foot, in the darkness, against the fatal invasion of necessity and of
baseness. There are noble and mysterious triumphs, which no eye
sees, which no renown rewards, which no flourish of trumpets
salutes. Life, misfortune, isolation, abandonment, poverty, are

battle-fields, which have their heroes,—heroes obscure, but sometimes greater than those who become illustrious. The Mason
should struggle in the same manner, and with the same bravery,
against those invasions of necessity and baseness, which come to
nations as well as to men. He should meet *them*, too, foot to foot,
even in the darkness, and protest against the national wrongs and
follies; against usurpation and the first inroads of that hydra,
Tyranny. There is no more sovereign eloquence than the truth in
indignation. It is more difficult for a people to keep than to gain
their freedom. The Protests of Truth are always needed. Continually, the right must protest against the fact. There is, in fact,
Eternity in the Right. The Mason should be the Priest and Soldier of that Right. If his country should be robbed of her liberties, he should still not despair. The protest of the Right against
the Fact persists forever. The robbery of a people never becomes
prescriptive. Reclamation of its rights is barred by no length of
time. Warsaw can no more be Tartar than Venice can be Teutonic.
A people may endure military usurpation, and subjugated States
kneel to States and wear the yoke, while under the stress of
necessity; but when the necessity disappears, if the people is fit to
be free, the submerged country will float to the surface and reappear,
and Tyranny be adjudged by History to have murdered its victims.

Whatever occurs, we should have Faith in the Justice and over-
ruling Wisdom of God, and Hope for the Future, and Loving-
kindness for those who are in error. God makes visible to men
His will in events; an obscure text, written in a mysterious language. Men make their translations of it forthwith, hasty, incorrect, full of faults, omissions, and misreadings. We see so short a
way along the arc of the great circle! Few minds comprehend
the Divine tongue. The most sagacious, the most calm, the most
profound, decipher the hieroglyphs slowly; and when they arrive
with their text, perhaps the need has long gone by; there are
already twenty translations in the public square—the most incorrect being, as of course, the most accepted and popular. From
each translation, a party is born; and from each misreading, a
faction. Each party believes or pretends that it has the only true
text, and each faction believes or pretends that it alone possesses
the light. Moreover, factions are blind men, who aim straight,
errors are excellent projectiles, striking skillfully, and with all the
violence that springs from false reasoning, wherever a want of logic

in those who defend the right, like a defect in a cuirass, makes them vulnerable.

Therefore it is that we shall often be discomfited in combatting error before the people. Antæus long resisted Hercules; and the heads of the Hydra grew as fast as they were cut off. It is absurd to say that *Error, wounded, writhes in pain, and dies amid her worshippers.* Truth conquers slowly. There is a wondrous vitality in Error. Truth, indeed, for the most part, shoots over the heads of the masses ; or if an error is prostrated for a moment, it is up again in a moment, and as vigorous as ever. It will not die when the brains are out, and the most stupid and irrational errors are the longest-lived.

Nevertheless, Masonry, which is Morality and Philosophy, must not cease to do its duty. We never know at what moment success awaits our efforts—generally when most unexpected—nor with what effect our efforts are or are not to be attended. Succeed or fail, Masonry must not bow to error, or succumb under discouragement. There were at Rome a few Carthaginian soldiers, taken prisoners, who refused to bow to Flaminius, and had a little of Hannibal's magnanimity. Masons should possess an equal greatness of soul. Masonry should be an energy ; finding its aim and effect in the amelioration of mankind. Socrates should enter into Adam, and produce Marcus Aurelius, in other words, bring forth from the man of enjoyments, the man of wisdom. Masonry should not be a mere watch-tower, built upon mystery, from which to gaze at ease upon the world, with no other result than to be a convenience for the curious. To hold the full cup of thought to the thirsty lips of men ; to give to all the true ideas of Deity ; to harmonize conscience and science, are the province of Philosophy. Morality is Faith in full bloom. Contemplation should lead to action, and the absolute be practical ; the ideal be made air and food and drink to the human mind. Wisdom is a sacred communion. It is only on that condition that it ceases to be a sterile love of Science, and becomes the one and supreme method by which to unite Humanity and arouse it to concerted action. Then Philosophy becomes Religion.

And Masonry, like History and Philosophy, has eternal duties— eternal, and, at the same time, simple—to oppose Caiaphas as Bishop, Draco or Jefferies as Judge, Trimalcion as Legislator, and Tiberius as Emperor. These are the symbols of the tyranny that degrades and crushes, and the corruption that defiles and it fbsts. In the works published for the use of the Craft we are told that the three great tenets of a Mason's profession, are Brotherly Love, Relief, and Truth. And it is true that a Brotherly affection and kindness should govern us in all our intercourse and relations with our brethren; and a generous and liberal philanthropy actuate us in regard to all men. To relieve the distressed is peculiarly the duty of Masons—a sacred duty, not to be omitted, neglected, or coldly or inefficiently complied with. It is also most true, that Truth is a Divine attribute and the foundation of every virtue. To be true, and to seek to find and learn the Truth, are the great objects of every good Mason.

As the Ancients did, Masonry styles Temperance, Fortitude, Prudence, and Justice, the four cardinal virtues. They are as necessary to nations as to individuals. The people that would be Free and Independent, must possess Sagacity, Forethought, Foresight, and careful Circumspection, all which are included in the meaning of the word Prudence. It must be temperate in asserting its rights, temperate in its councils, economical in its expenses; it must be bold, brave, courageous, patient under reverses, undismayed by disasters, hopeful amid calamities, like Rome when she sold the field at which Hannibal had his camp. No Cannæ or Pharsalia or Pavia or Agincourt or Waterloo must discourage her. Let her Senate sit in their seats until the Gauls pluck them by the beard. She must, above all things, be just, not truckling to the strong and warring on or plundering the weak; she must act on the square with all nations, and the feeblest tribes; always keeping her faith, honest in her legislation, upright in all her dealings. Whenever such a Republic exists, it will be immortal: for rashness, injustice, intemperance and luxury in prosperity, and despair and disorder in adversity, are the causes of the decay and dilapidation of nations.

II.

THE FELLOW-CRAFT.

In the Ancient Orient, all religion was more or less a mystery and there was no divorce from it of philosophy. The popular theology, taking the multitude of allegories and symbols for real·ities, degenerated into a worship of the celestial luminaries, of imaginary Deities with human feelings, passions, appetites, and lusts, of idols, stones, animals, reptiles. The Onion was sacred to the Egyptians, because its different layers were a symbol of the concentric heavenly spheres. Of course the popular religion could not satisfy the deeper longings and thoughts, the loftier aspirations of the Spirit, or the logic of reason. The first, therefore, was taught to the Initiated in the mysteries. There, also, it was taught by symbols. The vagueness of symbolism, capable of many inter-pretations, reached what the palpable and conventional creed could not. Its indefiniteness acknowledged the abstruseness of the subject: it treated that mysterious subject mystically: it endeav-ored to illustrate what it could not explain; to excite an appro-priate *feeling*, if it could not develop an adequate *idea ;* and to make the image a mere subordinate conveyance for the conception, which itself never became obvious or familiar.

Thus the knowledge now imparted by books and letters, was of old conveyed by symbols; and the priests invented or perpetuated a display of rites and exhibitions, which were not only more at-tractive to the eye than words, but often more suggestive and more pregnant with meaning to the mind.

Masonry, successor of the mysteries, still follows the ancient manner of teaching. Her ceremonies are like the ancient mystic shows,—not the reading of an essay, but the opening of a problem, requiring research, and constituting philosophy the arch-ex-pounder. Her symbols are the instruction she gives. The lectures are endeavors, often partial and one-sided, to interpret these sym-bols. He who would become an accomplished Mason must not be content merely to hear, or even to understand, the lectures; he

38

must, aided by them, and they having, as it were, marked out the way for him, study, interpret, and develop these symbols for himself.

* * * * * * * *

Though Masonry is identical with the ancient mysteries, it is so only in this qualified sense: that it presents but an imperfect image of their brilliancy, the ruins only of their grandeur, and a system that has experienced progressive alterations, the fruits of social events, political circumstances, and the ambitious imbecility of its improvers. After leaving Egypt, the mysteries were modified by the habits of the different nations among whom they were introduced, and especially by the religious systems of the countries into which they were transplanted. To maintain the established government, laws, and religion, was the obligation of the initiate everywhere; and everywhere they were the heritage of the priests, who were nowhere willing to make the common people co-proprietors with themselves of philosophical truth.

Masonry is not the Coliseum in ruins. It is rather a Roman palace of the middle ages, disfigured by modern architectural improvements, yet built on a Cyclopæan foundation laid by the Etruscans, and with many a stone of the superstructure taken from dwellings and temples of the age of Hadrian and Antoninus.

Christianity taught the doctrine of FRATERNITY; but repudiated that of political EQUALITY, by continually inculcating obedience to Cæsar, and to those lawfully in authority. Masonry was the first apostle of EQUALITY. In the Monastery there is *fraternity* and *equality*, but no *liberty*. Masonry added that also, and claimed for man the three-fold heritage, LIBERTY, EQUALITY, and FRATERNITY.

It was but a development of the original purpose of the mysteries, which was to teach men to know and practice their duties to themselves and their fellows, the great practical end of all philosophy and all knowledge.

Truths are the springs from which duties flow; and it is but a few hundred years since a new Truth began to be distinctly seen; that MAN IS SUPREME OVER INSTITUTIONS, AND NOT THEY OVER HIM. Man has *natural* empire over *all* institutions. They are for him, according to his development; not he for them. This seems to us a very simple statement, one to which all men, everywhere, ought to assent. But once it was a great new Truth,—not revealed until governments had been in existence for at least five thousand years. Once revealed, it imposed new duties on men. Man owed it to *himself* to be free. He owed it to his *country* to seek to give *her* freedom, or maintain her in that possession. It made Tyranny and Usurpation the enemies of the Human Race. It created a general outlawry of Despots and Despotisms, temporal and spiritual. The sphere of Duty was immensely enlarged. Patriotism had, henceforth, a new and wider meaning. Free Government, Free Thought, Free Conscience, Free Speech! All these came to be inalienable rights, which those who had parted with them or been robbed of them, or whose ancestors had lost them, had the right summarily to retake. Unfortunately, as Truths always become perverted into falsehoods, and are falsehoods when misapplied, *this* Truth became the Gospel of Anarchy, soon after it was first preached.

Masonry early comprehended this Truth, and recognized its own enlarged duties. Its symbols then came to have a wider meaning; but it also assumed the mask of Stone-masonry, and borrowed its working-tools, and so was supplied with new and apt symbols. It aided in bringing about the French Revolution, disappeared with the Girondists, was born again with the restoration of order, and sustained Napoleon, because, though Emperor, he acknowledged the right of the people to select its rulers, and was at the head of a nation refusing to receive back its old kings. He pleaded, with sabre, musket, and cannon, the great cause of the People against Royalty, the right of the French people even to make a Corsican General their Emperor, if it pleased them.

Masonry felt that this Truth had the Omnipotence of God on its side; and that neither Pope nor Potentate could overcome it. It was a truth dropped into the world's wide treasury, and forming a part of the heritage which each generation receives, enlarges, and holds in trust, and of necessity bequeaths to mankind; the personal estate of man, entailed of nature to the end of time. And Masonry early recognized it as true, that to set forth and develope a truth, or any human excellence of gift or growth, is to greaten the spiritual glory of the race; that whosoever aids the march of a Truth, and makes the thought a thing, writes in the same line with Moses, and with Him who died upon the cross; and has an intellectual sympathy with the Deity himself.

The best gift we can bestow on man is manhood. It is that

which Masonry is ordained of God to bestow on its votaries: not sectarianism and religious dogma; not a rudimental morality, that may be found in the writings of Confucius, Zoroaster, Seneca, and the Rabbis, in the Proverbs and Ecclesiastes; not a little and cheap common-school knowledge; but manhood and science and philosophy.

Not that Philosophy or Science is in opposition to Religion. For Philosophy is but that knowledge of God and the Soul, which is derived from observation of the manifested action of God and the Soul, and from a wise analogy. It is the intellectual guide which the religious sentiment needs. The true religious philosophy of an imperfect being, is not a system of creed, but, as SOCRATES thought, an infinite search or approximation. Philosophy is that intellectual and moral progress, which the religious sentiment inspires and ennobles.

As to Science, it could not walk alone, while religion was stationary. It consists of those matured inferences from experience which all other experience confirms. It realizes and unites all that was truly valuable in both the old schemes of mediation,—one heroic, or the system of action and effort; and the mystical theory of spiritual, contemplative communion. "Listen to me," says GALEN, "as to the voice of the Eleusinian Hierophant, and believe that the study of Nature is a mystery no less important than theirs, nor less adapted to display the wisdom and power of the Great Creator. Their lessons and demonstrations were obscure, but ours are clear and unmistakable."

We deem that to be the best knowledge we can obtain of the Soul of another man, which is furnished by his actions and his life-long conduct. Evidence to the contrary, supplied by what another man informs us that this Soul has said to his, would weigh little against the former. The first Scriptures for the human race were written by God on the Earth and Heavens. The reading of these Scriptures is Science. Familiarity with the grass and trees, the insects and the infusoria, teaches us deeper lessons of love and faith, than we can glean from the writings of FÉNÉLON and AUGUSTINE. The great Bible of God is ever open before mankind.

Knowledge is convertible into power, and axioms into rules of utility and duty. But knowledge itself is not Power. Wisdom is Power; and her Prime Minister is JUSTICE, which is the perfected law of TRUTH. The purpose, therefore, of Education and Science

41

is to make a man wise. If knowledge does not make him so, it is wasted, like water poured on the sands. To know the *formulas* of Masonry, is of as little value, by itself, as to know so many words and sentences in some barbarous African or Australasian dialect. To know even the *meaning* of the symbols, is but little, unless that adds to our wisdom, and also to our charity, which is to justice like one hemisphere of the brain to the other.

Do not lose sight, then, of the true object of your studies in Masonry. It is to add to your estate of wisdom, and not merely to your knowledge. A man may spend a lifetime in studying a single specialty of knowledge,—botany, conchology, or entomology, for instance,—in committing to memory names derived from the Greek, and classifying and reclassifying; and yet be no wiser than when he began. It is the great truths as to all that most concerns a man, as to his rights, interests, and duties, that Masonry seeks to teach her initiates.

The wiser a man becomes, the less will he be inclined to submit tamely to the imposition of fetters or a yoke, on his conscience or his person. For, by increase of wisdom he not only better *knows* his rights, but the more highly *values* them, and is more conscious of his worth and dignity. His pride then urges him to assert his independence. He becomes better *able* to assert it also; and better able to assist others or his country, when they or she stake all, even existence, upon the same assertion. But mere knowledge makes no one independent, nor fits him to be free. It often only makes him a more useful slave. Liberty is a curse to the ignorant and brutal.

Political science has for its object to ascertain in what manner and by means of what institutions political and personal freedom may be secured and perpetuated: not license, or the mere right of every man to vote, but entire and absolute freedom of thought and opinion, alike free of the despotism of monarch and mob and prelate; freedom of action within the limits of the general law enacted for all; the Courts of Justice, with impartial Judges and juries, open to all alike; weakness and poverty equally potent in those Courts as power and wealth; the avenues to office and honor open alike to all the worthy; the military powers, *in war or peace*, in strict subordination to the civil power; arbitrary arrests for acts not known to the law as crimes, impossible; Romish Inquisitions, Star-Chambers, Military Commissions, unknown ; the means of instruction within reach of the children of all; the right of Free Speech; and accountability of all public officers, civil and military.

If Masonry needed to be justified for imposing political as well as moral duties on its initiates, it would be enough to point to the sad history of the world. It would not even need that she should turn back the pages of history to the chapters written by Tacitus: that she should recite the incredible horrors of despotism under Caligula and Domitian, Caracalla and Commodus, Vitellius and Maximin. She need only point to the centuries of calamity through which the gay French nation passed; to the long oppression of the feudal ages, of the selfish Bourbon kings; to those times when the peasants were robbed and slaughtered by their own lords and princes, like sheep; when the lord claimed the first-fruits of the peasant's marriage-bed; when the captured city was given up to merciless rape and massacre; when the State-prisons groaned with innocent victims, and the Church blessed the banners of pitiless murderers, and sang Te Deums for the crowning mercy of the Eve of St. Bartholomew.

We might turn over the pages, to a later chapter,—that of the reign of the Fifteenth Louis, when young girls, hardly more than children, were kidnapped to serve his lusts; when *lettres de cachet* filled the Bastille with persons accused of no crime, with husbands who were in the way of the pleasures of lascivious wives and of villains wearing orders of nobility; when the people were ground between the upper and the nether millstone of taxes, customs, and excises; and when the Pope's Nuncio and the Cardinal de la Roche-Ayman, devoutly kneeling, one on each side of Madame du Barry, the king's abandoned prostitute, put the slippers on her naked feet, as she rose from the adulterous bed. Then, indeed, suffering and toil were the two forms of man, and the people were but beasts of burden.

The true Mason is he who labors strenuously to help his Order effect its great purposes. Not that the Order can effect them by itself; but that it, too, can help. It also is one of God's instruments. It is a Force and a Power; and shame upon it, if it did not exert itself, and if need be, sacrifice its children in the cause of humanity, as Abraham was ready to offer up Isaac on the altar of sacrifice. It will not forget that noble allegory of Curtius leaping, all in armor, into the great yawning gulf that opened to swallow Rome. It will TRY. It shall not be *its* fault if the day *never* comes when man will no longer have to fear a conquest, an invasion, a usurpation, a rivalry of nations with the armed hand, an interruptior of civilization depending on a marriage-royal, or a birth in the hereditary tyrannies; a partition of the peoples by a Congress, a dismemberment by the downfall of a dynasty, a com bat of two religions, meeting head to head, like two goats of dark- ness on the bridge of the Infinite: when they will no longer have to fear famine, spoliation, prostitution from distress, misery from lack of work, and all the brigandages of chance in the forest of events: when nations will gravitate about the Truth, like stars about the light, each in its own orbit, without clashing or collision; and everywhere Freedom, cinctured with stars, crowned with the celestial splendors, and with wisdom and justice on either hand, will reign supreme.

In your studies as a Fellow-Craft you must be guided by REA- SON, LOVE, and FAITH.

We do not now discuss the differences between Reason and Faith, and undertake to define the domain of each. But it is necessary to say, that even in the ordinary affairs of life we are governed far more by what we *believe* than by what we *know ;* by FAITH and ANALOGY, than by REASON. The "Age of Reason" of the French Revolution taught, we know, what a folly it is to enthrone Reason by itself as supreme. Reason is at fault when it deals with the Infinite. There we must revere and believe. Not- withstanding the calamities of the virtuous, the miseries of the deserving, the prosperity of tyrants and the murder of martyrs, we *must* believe there is a wise, just, merciful, and loving God, an Intelligence and a Providence, supreme over all, and caring for the minutest things and events. A Faith is a necessity to man. Woe to him who believes nothing!

We believe that the soul of another is of a certain nature and possesses certain qualities, that he is generous and honest, or pe- nurious and knavish, that she is virtuous and amiable, or vicious and ill-tempered, from the countenance alone, from little more than a glimpse of it, without the means of *knowing.* We venture our fortune on the signature of a man on the other side of the world, whom we never saw, upon the belief that he is honest and trustworthy. We believe that occurrences have taken place, upon the assertion of others. We believe that one will acts upor another, and in the reality of a multitude of other phenomena, that Reason cannot explain.

But we ought *not* to believe what Reason authoritatively denies, fnat at which the sense of right revolts, that which is absurd or self-contradictory, or at issue with experience or science, or that which degrades the character of the Deity, and would make Him revengeful, malignant, cruel, or unjust.

A man's Faith is as much his own as his Reason is. His Freedom consists as much in his faith being free as in his will being uncontrolled by power. All the Priests and Augurs of Rome or Greece had not the right to require Cicero or Socrates to believe in the absurd mythology of the vulgar. All the Imaums of Mohammedanism have not the right to require a Pagan to believe that Gabriel dictated the Koran to the Prophet. All the Brahmins that ever lived, if assembled in one conclave like the Cardinals, could not gain a right to compel a single human being to believe in the Hindu Cosmogony. No man or body of men *can* be infallible, and authorized to decide what other men shall believe, as to any tenet of faith. Except to those who first receive it, every religion and the truth of all inspired writings depend on *human* testimony and internal evidences, to be judged of by Reason and the wise analogies of Faith. Each man must necessarily have the right to judge of their truth for himself; because no one man can have any higher or better right to judge than another of equal information and intelligence.

Domitian claimed to be the Lord God; and statues and images of him, in silver and gold, filled almost the whole world. He claimed to be regarded as the God of all men; and, according to Suetonius, began his letters thus: " *Our Lord and God commands that it should be done so and so ;*" and formally decreed that no one should address him otherwise, either in writing or by word of mouth. Palfurius Sura, the philosopher, who was his chief delator, accusing those who refused to recognize his divinity, however much *he* may have believed in that divinity, had not the right to demand that a single Christian in Rome or the provinces should do the same.

Reason is far from being the only guide, in morals or in political science. Love or loving-kindness must keep it company, to exclude fanaticism, intolerance, and persecution, to all of which a morality too ascetic, and extreme political principles, invariably lead. We must also have faith in ourselves, and in our fellows and the people. or we shall be easily discouraged by reverses, and oui ardor cooled by obstacles. We must not listen to Reason alone. Force comes more from Faith and Love: and it is by the aid of these that man scales the loftiest heights of morality, or becomes the Saviour and Redeemer of a People. Reason must hold the helm; but these supply the motive power. They are the wings of the soul. Enthusiasm is generally unreasoning; and without it, and Love and Faith. there would have been no RIENZI, or TELL, or SYDNEY, or any other of the great patriots whose names are immortal. If the Deity had been merely and only All-wise and All-mighty, He would never have created the universe.

       *   *   *   *   *   *

It is GENIUS that gets Power; and its prime lieutenants are FORCE and WISDOM. The unruliest of men bend before the leader that has the sense to see and the will to do. It is Genius that rules with God-like Power; that unveils, with its counsellors, the hidden human mysteries, cuts asunder with its word the huge knots, and builds up with its word the crumbled ruins. At its glance fall down the senseless idols, whose altars have been on all the high places and in all the sacred groves. Dishonesty and imbecility stand abashed before it. Its single Yea or Nay revokes the wrongs of ages, and is heard among the future generations. Its power is immense, because its wisdom is immense. Genius is the Sun of the political sphere. Force and Wisdom, its ministers, are the orbs that carry its light into darkness, and answer it with their solid reflecting Truth.

Development is symbolized by the use of the Mallet and Chisel, the development of the energies and intellect, of the individual and the people. Genius may place itself at the head of an unintellectual, uneducated, unenergetic nation; but in a free country, to cultivate the intellect of those who elect, is the only mode of securing intellect and genius for rulers. The world is seldom ruled by the great spirits, except after dissolution and new birth.. In periods of transition and convulsion, the Long Parliaments, the Robespierres and Marats, and the semi-respectabilities of intellect, too often hold the reins of power. The Cromwells and Napoleons come later. After Marius and Sylla and Cicero the rhetorician, CÆSAR. The great intellect is often too sharp for the granite of this life. Legislators may be very ordinary men; for legislation is very ordinary work; it is but the final issue of a million minds.

The power of the purse or the sword, compared to that of the spirit, is poor and contemptible. As to *lands*, you may have agrarian laws, and equal partition. But a man's intellect is all his own, held direct from God, an inalienable fief. It is the most potent of weapons in the hands of a Paladin. If the people comprehend Force in the physical sense, how much more do they reverence the intellectual! Ask Hildebrand, or Luther, or Loyola. They fall prostrate before it, as before an idol. The mastery of mind over mind is the only conquest worth having. The other injures both, and dissolves at a breath ; rude as it is, the great cable falls down and snaps at last. But this dimly resembles the dominion of the Creator. It does not need a subject like that of Peter the Hermit. If the stream be but bright and strong, it will sweep like a spring-tide to the popular heart. Not in word only, but in intellectual act lies the fascination. It is the homage to the Invisible. This power, knotted with Love, is the golden chain let down into the well of Truth, or the invisible chain that binds the ranks of mankind together.

Influence of man over man is a law of nature, whether it be by a great estate in land or in intellect. It may mean slavery, a deference to the eminent human judgment. Society hangs spiritually together, like the revolving spheres above. The free country, in which intellect and genius govern, will endure. Where they serve, and other influences govern, the national life is short. All the nations that have tried to govern themselves by their smallest, by the incapables, or merely respectables, have come to nought. Constitutions and Laws, without Genius and Intellect to govern, will not prevent decay. In that case they have the dry-rot and the life dies out of them by degrees.

To give a nation the franchise of the Intellect is the only sure mode of perpetuating freedom. This will compel exertion and generous care for the people from those on the higher seats, and honorable and intelligent allegiance from those below. Then political public life will protect all men from self-abasement in sensual pursuits, from vulgar acts and low greed, by giving the noble ambition of just imperial rule. To elevate the people by teaching loving-kindness and wisdom, with power to him that teaches best; and so to develop the free State from the rough ashlar;--this

3

is the great labor in which Masonry desires to lend a helping hand.

All of us should labor in building up the great monument of a nation, the Holy House of the Temple. The cardinal virtues must not be partitioned among men, becoming the exclusive property of some, like the common crafts. ALL are apprenticed to the partners, Duty and Honor.

Masonry is a march and a struggle toward the Light. For the individual as well as the nation, Light is Virtue, Manliness, Intelligence, Liberty. Tyranny over the soul or body, is darkness. The freest people, like the freest man, is always in danger of re-lapsing into servitude. Wars are almost always fatal to Republics They create tyrants, and consolidate their power. They spring, for the most part, from evil counsels. When the small and the base are intrusted with power, legislation and administration become but two parallel series of errors and blunders, ending in war, calamity, and the necessity for a tyrant. When the nation feels its feet sliding backward, as if it walked on the ice, the time has come for a supreme effort. The magnificent tyrants of the past are but the types of those of the future. Men and nations will always sell themselves into slavery, to gratify their passions and obtain revenge. The tyrant's plea, necessity, is always available; and the tyrant once in power, the necessity of providing for his safety makes him savage. Religion is a power, and he must control that. Independent, its sanctuaries might rebel. Then it becomes unlawful for the people to worship God in their own way, and the old spiritual despotisms revive. Men must believe as Power wills, or die; and even if they may believe as they will, all they have, lands, houses, body, and soul, are stamped with the royal brand. *"I am the State,"* said Louis the Fourteenth to his peasants; *"the very shirts on your backs are mine, and I can take them if I will."*

And dynasties so established endure, like that of the Cæsars of Rome, of the Cæsars of Constantinople, of the Caliphs, the Stuarts, the Spaniards, the Goths, the Valois, until the race wears out, and ends with lunatics and idiots, who *still* rule. There is no concord among men, to end the horrible bondage. The State falls inwardly, as well as by the outward blows of the incoherent elements. The furious human passions, the sleeping human indolence, the stolid human ignorance, the rivalry of human castes, are as good for the kings as the swords of the Paladins. The worshippers have all bowed so long to the old idol, th; t they cannot go into the streets and choose another Grand Llama. And so the effete State floats on down the puddled stream of Time, until the tempest or the tidal sea discovers that the worm has consumed its strength, and it crumbles into oblivion.

     *   *   *   *   *   *

Civil and religious Freedom must go hand in hand ; and Persecution matures them both. A people content with the thoughts made for them by the priests of a church will be content with Royalty by Divine Right,—the Church and the Throne mutually sustaining each other. They will smother schism and reap infidelity and indifference ; and while the battle for freedom goes on around them, they will only sink the more apathetically into servitude and a deep trance, perhaps occasionally interrupted by furious fits of frenzy, followed by helpless exhaustion.

Despotism is not difficult in any land that has only known one master from its childhood ; but there is no harder problem than to perfect and perpetuate free government by the people themselves; for it is not one king that is needed: all must be kings. It is easy to set up Masaniello, that in a few days he may fall lower than before. But free government grows slowly, like the individual human faculties ; and like the forest-trees, from the inner heart outward. Liberty is not only the common birth-right, but it is lost as well by non-user as by mis-user. It depends far more on the universal effort than any other human property. It has no single shrine or holy well of pilgrimage for the nation ; for its waters should burst out freely from the whole soil.

The free popular power is one that is only known in its strength in the hour of adversity ; for all its trials, sacrifices and expectations are its own. It is trained to think for itself, and also to act for itself. When the enslaved people prostrate themselves in the dust before the hurricane, like the alarmed beasts of the field, the free people stand erect before it, in all the strength of unity, in self-reliance, in mutual reliance, with effrontery against all but the visible hand of God. It is neither cast down by calamity nor elated by success.

This vast power of endurance, of forbearance, of patience, and of performance, is only acquired by continual exercise of all the functions, like the healthful physical human vigor, like the individual moral vigor.

And the maxim is no less true than old, that eternal vigilance is
the prize of liberty. It is curious to observe the universal pretext
by which the tyrants of all times take away the national liberties.
It is stated in the statutes of Edward II., that the justices and the
sheriff should no longer be elected by the people, on account of the
riots and dissensions which had arisen. The same reason was given
long before for the suppression of popular election of the bishops :
and there is a witness to this untruth in the yet older times, when
Rome lost her freedom, and her indignant citizens declared that
tumultuous liberty is better than disgraceful tranquillity.

   *   *   *   *   *   *

With the Compass and Scale, we can trace all the figures used
in the mathematics of planes, or in what are called GEOMETRY
and TRIGONOMETRY, two words that are themselves deficient
in meaning. GEOMETRY, which the letter G. in most Lodges is
said to signify, means measurement of land or the earth—or Sur-
veying; and TRIGONOMETRY, the measurement of triangles, or
figures with three sides or angles. The latter is by far the most
appropriate name for the science intended to be expressed by the
word "Geometry." Neither is of a meaning sufficiently wide:
for although the vast surveys of great spaces of the earth's surface, and of coasts, by which shipwreck and calamity to mariners
are avoided, are effected by means of triangulation;—though it
was by the same method that the French astronomers measured a
degree of latitude and so established a scale of measures on an
immutable basis; though it is by means of the immense triangle
that has for its base a line drawn in imagination between the place
of the earth now and its place six months hence in space, and for
its apex a planet or star, that the distance of Jupiter or Sirius from
the earth is ascertained; and though there is a triangle still more
vast, its base extending either way from us, with and past the
horizon into immensity, and its apex infinitely distant above us;
to which corresponds a similar infinite triangle below—what is
above equalling what is below, immensity equalling immensity ;—
yet the Science of Numbers, to which Pythagoras attached so much
importance, and whose mysteries are found everywhere in the
ancient religions, and most of all in the Kabalah and the Bible, is
not sufficiently expressed by either the word " Geometry" or the
word "Trigonometry." For that science includes these, with Arith-
metic, and also with Algebra, Logarithms, the Integral and Differ-

ential Calculus; and by means of it are worked out the great problems of Astronomy or the Laws of the Stars.

♦ * * * * *

Virtue is out heroic bravery, to *do* the thing thought to be true, in spite of all enemies of flesh or spirit, in despite of all temptations or menaces. Man is accountable for the *up*rightness of his doctrine, but not for the rightness of it. Devout enthusiasm is far easier than a good action. The end of thought is action; the sole purpose of Religion is an Ethic. Theory, in political science, is worthless, except for the purpose of being realized in practice.

In every *credo*, religious or political, as in the soul of man, there are two regions, the Dialectic and the Ethic; and it is only when the two are harmoniously blended, that a perfect discipline is evolved. There are men who dialectically are Christians, as there are a multitude who dialectically are Masons, and yet who are ethically Infidels, as these are ethically of the Profane, in the strictest sense :—intellectual believers, but practical atheists:— men who will write you "Evidences," in perfect faith in their logic, but cannot carry out the Christian or Masonic doctrine, owing to the strength, or weakness, of the flesh. On the other hand, there are many dialectical skeptics, but ethical believers, as there are many Masons who have never undergone initiation ; and as ethics are the end and purpose of religion, so are ethical believers the most worthy. He that *does* right is better than he that *thinks* right.

But you must not act upon the hypothesis that all men are hypocrites, whose conduct does not square with their sentiments. No vice is more rare, for no task is more difficult, than systematic hypocrisy. When the Demagogue becomes a Usurper it does not follow that he was all the time a hypocrite. Shallow men only so judge of others.

The truth is, that creed has, in general, very little influence on the conduct; in religion, on that of the individual; in politics, on that of party. As a general thing, the Mahometan, in the Orient, is far more honest and trustworthy than the Christian. A Gospel of Love in the mouth, is an Avatar of Persecution in the heart. Men who believe in eternal damnation and a literal sea of fire and brimstone, incur the certainty of it, according to their creed, on the slightest temptation of appetite or passion. Predestination insists on the necessity of good works. In Masonry, at the least flow of passion, one speaks ill of another behind his back ; and so far from the "Brotherhood" of Blue Masonry being real, and the solemn pledges contained in the use of the word "Brother" being complied with, extraordinary pains are taken to show that Masonry is a sort of abstraction, which scorns to interfere in worldly matters. The rule may be regarded as universal, that, where there is a choice to be made, a Mason will give his vote and influence, in politics and business, to the less qualified profane in preference to the better qualified Mason. One will take an oath to oppose any unlawful usurpation of power, and then become the ready and even eager instrument of a usurper. Another will call one "Brother," and then play toward him the part of Judas Iscariot, or strike him, as Joab did Abner, under the fifth rib, with a lie whose authorship is not to be traced. Masonry does not change human nature, and cannot make honest men out of born knaves.

While you are still engaged in preparation, and in accumulating principles for future use, do not forget the words of the Apostle James: "For if any be a hearer of the word, and not a doer, he is like unto a man beholding his natural face in a glass, for he beholdeth himself, and goeth away, and straightway forgetteth what manner of man he was; but whoso looketh into the perfect law of liberty, and continueth, he being not a forgetful hearer, but a doer of the work, this man shall be blessed in his work. If any man among you seem to be religious, and bridleth not his tongue, but deceiveth his own heart, this man's religion is vain. . . . Faith, if it hath not works, is dead, being an abstraction. A man is justified by works, and not by faith only. . . . The devils believe,—and tremble. . . . As the body without the heart is dead, so is faith without works."

      *   *   *   *   *   *

In political science, also, free governments are erected and free constitutions framed, upon some simple and intelligible theory. Upon whatever theory they are based, no sound conclusion is to be reached except by carrying the theory out without flinching, both in argument on constitutional questions and in practice. Shrink from the true theory through timidity, or wander from it through want of the logical faculty, or transgress against it through passion or on the plea of necessity or expediency, and you have denial or invasion of rights, laws that offend against first principles, usurpation of illegal powers, or abnegation and abdication of legitimate authority.

Do not forget, either, that as the showy, superficial, impudent and self-conceited will almost always be preferred, even in utmost stress of danger and calamity of the State, to the man of solid learning, large intellect, and catholic sympathies, because he is nearer the common popular and legislative level, so the highest truth is not acceptable to the mass of mankind.

When SOLON was asked if he had given his countrymen the best laws, he answered, " *The best they are capable of receiving.*" This is one of the profoundest utterances on record; and yet like all great truths, so simple as to be rarely comprehended. It contains the whole philosophy of History. It utters a truth which, had it been recognized, would have saved men an immensity of vain, idle disputes, and have led them into the clearer paths of knowledge in the Past. It means this,—that all truths are *Truths of Period,* and not truths for eternity; that whatever great fact has had strength and vitality enough to make itself real, whether of religion, morals, government, or of whatever else, and to find place in this world, has been a truth *for the time, and as good as men were capable of receiving.*

So, too, with great men. The intellect and capacity of a people has a single measure,—that of the great men whom Providence gives it, and whom it *receives.* There have always been men too great for their time or their people. Every people makes *such* men only its idols, as it is capable of comprehending.

To impose ideal truth or law upon an incapable and merely *real* man, must ever be a vain and empty speculation. The laws of sympathy govern in this as they do in regard to men who are put at the head. We do not know, as yet, what qualifications the sheep insist on in a leader. With men who are too high intellectually, the mass have as little sympathy as they have with the stars. When BURKE, the wisest statesman England ever had, rose to speak, the House of Commons was depopulated as upon an agreed signal. There is as little sympathy between the mass and the highest TRUTHS. The highest truth, being incomprehensible to the man of realities, as the highest man is, and largely above his level, will be a great unreality and falsehood to an unintellectual man. The profoundest doctrines of Christianity and Philosophy would be mere jargon and babble to a Potawatomie Indian. The popular explanations of the symbols of Masonry are fitting for the multitude that have swarmed into the Temples,—being fully up to the level

of their capacity. Catholicism was a vital truth in its earliest ages
but it became obsolete, and Protestantism arose, flourished, and
deteriorated. The doctrines of ZOROASTER were the best which
the ancient Persians were fitted to receive; those of CONFUCIUS
were fitted for the Chinese; those of MOHAMMED for the idolatrous
Arabs of his age. Each was Truth for the time. Each was a
GOSPEL, preached by a REFORMER; and if any men are so little
fortunate as to remain content therewith, when others have attained a higher truth, it is their misfortune and not their fault.
They are to be pitied for it, and not persecuted.

Do not expect easily to convince men of the truth, or to lead
them to think aright. The subtle human intellect can weave its
mists over even the clearest vision. Remember that it is eccentric
enough to ask unanimity from a jury; but to ask it from any
large number of men on any point of political faith is amazing.
You can hardly get two men in any Congress or Convention to
agree;—nay, you can rarely get one to agree with *himself.* The
political church which chances to be supreme anywhere has an
indefinite number of tongues. How then can we expect men to
agree as to matters beyond the cognizance of the senses? How
can we compass the Infinite and the Invisible with any chain of
evidence? Ask the small sea-waves what they murmur among
the pebbles! How many of those words that come from the invisible shore are lost, like the birds, in the long passage? How vainly
do we strain the eyes across the long Infinite! We must be content, as the children are, with the pebbles that have been stranded,
since it is forbidden us to explore the hidden depths.

The Fellow-Craft is especially taught by this not to become
wise in his own conceit. Pride in unsound theories is worse than
ignorance. Humility becomes a Mason. Take some quiet, sober
moment of life, and add together the two ideas of Pride and Man;
behold him, creature of a span, stalking through infinite space in
all the grandeur of littleness! Perched on a speck of the universe,
every wind of Heaven strikes into his blood the coldness of death;
his soul floats away from his body like the melody from the string.
Day and night, like dust on the wheel, he is rolled along the heavens, through a labyrinth of worlds, and all the creations of God are
flaming on every side, further than even his imagination can reach.
Is this a creature to make for himself a crown of glory, to deny his
own flesh, to mock at his fellow, sprung with him from that drst

to which both will soon return? Does the proud man not err?
Does he not suffer? Does he not die? When he reasons, is he
never stopped short by difficulties? When he acts, does he never
succumb to the temptations of pleasure? When he lives, is he free
from pain? Do the diseases not claim him as their prey? When
he dies, can he escape the common grave? Pride is not the heritage of man. Humility should dwell with frailty, and atone for
ignorance, error, and imperfection.

Neither should the Mason be over-anxious for office and honor,
however certainly he may feel that he has the capacity to serve the
State. He should neither seek nor spurn honors. It is good to
enjoy the blessings of fortune; it is better to submit without a
pang to their loss. The greatest deeds are not done in the glare of
light, and before the eyes of the populace. He whom God has
gifted with a love of retirement possesses, as it were, an additional
sense; and among the vast and noble scenes of nature, we find the
balm for the wounds we have received among the pitiful shifts of
policy; for the attachment to solitude is the surest preservative
from the ills of life.

But Resignation is the more noble in proportion as it is the less
passive. Retirement is only a morbid selfishness, if it prohibit
exertions for others; as it is only dignified and noble, when it is
the shade whence the oracles issue that are to instruct mankind;
and retirement of this nature is the sole seclusion which a good
and wise man will covet or commend. The very philosophy which
makes such a man covet the *quiet*, will make him eschew the *inu-
tility* of the hermitage. Very little praiseworthy would Lord
BOLINGBROKE have seemed among his haymakers and ploughmen,
if among haymakers and ploughmen he had looked with an indifferent eye upon a profligate minister and a venal Parliament.
Very little interest would have attached to his beans and vetches,
if beans and vetches had caused him to forget that if he was hap-
pier on a farm he could be more useful in a Senate, and made him
forego, in the sphere of a bailiff, all care for re-entering that of a
legislator.

Remember, also, that there is an education which quickens the
intellect, and leaves the heart hollower or harder than before.
There are ethical lessons in the laws of the heavenly bodies, in the
properties of earthly elements, in geography, chemistry, geology,
and all the material sciences. Things are symbols of Truths.

Properties are symbols of Truths. Science, not teaching moral and spiritual truths, is dead and dry, of little more real value than to commit to the memory a long row of unconnected dates, or of the names of bugs or butterflies.

Christianity, it is said, begins from the burning of the false gods by the people themselves. Education begins with the burning of our intellectual and moral idols: our prejudices, notions, conceits, our worthless or ignoble purposes. Especially it is necessary to shake off the love of worldly gain. With Freedom comes the longing for worldly advancement. In that race men are ever falling, rising, running, and falling again. The lust for wealth and the abject dread of poverty delve the furrows on many a noble brow. The gambler grows old as he watches the chances. Lawful hazard drives Youth away before its time; and this Youth draws heavy bills of exchange on Age. Men live, like the engines, at high pressure, a hundred years in a hundred months; the ledger becomes the Bible, and the day-book the Book of the Morning Prayer.

Hence flow overreachings and sharp practice, heartless traffic in which the capitalist buys profit with the lives of the laborers, speculations that coin a nation's agonies into wealth, and all the other devilish enginery of Mammon. This, and greed for office, are the two columns at the entrance to the Temple of Moloch. It is doubtful whether the latter, blossoming in falsehood, trickery, and fraud, is not even more pernicious than the former. At all events they are twins, and fitly mated; and as either gains control of the unfortunate subject, his soul withers away and decays, and at last dies out. The souls of half the human race leave them long before they die. The two greeds are twin plagues of the leprosy, and make the man unclean; and whenever they break out they spread until "they cover all the skin of him that hath the plague, from his head even to his foot." Even the raw flesh of the heart becomes unclean with it.

    *   *   *   *   *   *

Alexander of Macedon has left a saying behind him which has survived his conquests: "*Nothing is nobler than work.*" Work only can keep even kings respectable. And when a king is a king indeed, it is an honorable office to give tone to the manners and morals of a nation; to set the example of virtuous conduct, and restore in spirit the old schools of chivalry, in which the young manhood may be nurtured to real greatness. Work and wages *will* go together in men's minds, in the most royal institutions. We must ever come to the idea of real work. The rest that follows labor should be sweeter than the rest which follows rest.

Let no Fellow-Craft imagine that the work of the lowly and uninfluential is not worth the doing. There is no legal limit to the possible influences of a good deed or a wise word or a generous effort. Nothing is really small. Whoever is open to the deep penetration of nature knows this. Although, indeed, no absolute satisfaction may be vouchsafed to philosophy, any more in circumscribing the cause than in limiting the effect, the man of thought and contemplation falls into unfathomable ecstacies in view of all the decompositions of forces resulting in unity. All works for all. Destruction is not annihilation, but regeneration.

Algebra applies to the clouds; the radiance of the star benefits the rose; no thinker would dare to say that the perfume of the hawthorn is useless to the constellations. Who, then, can calculate the path of the molecule? How do we know that the creations of worlds are not determined by the fall of grains of sand? Who, then, understands the reciprocal flow and ebb of the infinitely great and the infinitely small; the echoing of causes in the abysses of beginning, and the avalanches of creation? A flesh-worm is of account; the small is great; the great is small; all is in equilibrium in necessity. There are marvellous relations between beings and things; in this inexhaustible Whole, from sun to grub, there is no scorn: all need each other. Light does not carry terrestrial perfumes into the azure depths, without knowing what it does with them; night distributes the stellar essence to the sleeping plants. Every bird which flies has the thread of the Infinite in its claw. Germination includes the hatching of a meteor, and the tap of a swallow's bill, breaking the egg; and it leads forward the birth of an earth-worm and the advent of a Socrates. Where the telescope ends the microscope begins. Which of them the grander view? A bit of mould is a Pleiad of flowers—a nebula is an ant-hill of stars.

There is the same and a still more wonderful interpenetration between the things of the intellect and the things of matter. Elements and principles are mingled, combined, espoused, multiplied one by another, to such a degree as to bring the material world and the moral world into the same light. Phenomena are perpetually folded back upon themselves. In the vast cosmical changes the universal life comes and goes in unknown quantities, enveloping all in the invisible mystery of the emanations, losing no dream from no single sleep, sowing an animalcule here, crumbling a star there, oscillating, and winding in curves; making a force of Light, and an element of Thought; disseminated and indivisible, dissolving all save that point without length, breadth, or thickness, The MYSELF; reducing everything to the Soul-atom; making everything blossom into God; entangling all activities, from the highest to the lowest, in the obscurity of a dizzying mechanism; hanging the flight of an insect upon the movement of the earth; subordinating, perhaps, if only by the identity of the law, the eccentric evolutions of the comet in the firmament, to the whirlings of the infusoria in the drop of water. A mechanism made of mind, the first motor of which is the gnat, and its last wheel the zodiac.

A peasant-boy, guiding Bülow by the right one of two roads, the other being impassable for artillery, enables him to reach Waterloo in time to save Wellington from a defeat that would have been a rout; and so enables the kings to imprison Napoleon on a barren rock in mid-ocean. An unfaithful smith, by slovenly shoeing of a horse, causes his lameness, and, he stumbling, the career of his world-conquering rider ends, and the destinies of empires are changed. A generous officer permits an imprisoned monarch to end his game of chess before leading him to the block; and meanwhile the usurper dies, and the prisoner reascends the throne. An unskillful workman repairs the compass, or malice or stupidity disarranges it, the ship mistakes her course, the waves swallow a Cæsar, and a new chapter is written in the history of a world. What we call accident is but the adamantine chain of indissoluble connection between all created things. The locust, hatched in the Arabian sands, the small worm that destroys the cotton-boll, one making famine in the Orient, the other closing the mills and starving the workmen and their children in the Occident, with riots and massacres, are as much the ministers of God as the earthquake; and the fate of nations depends more on them than on the intellect of its kings and legislators. A civil war in America will end in shaking the world; and that war may be caused by the vote of some ignorant prize-fighter or crazed fanatic in a city or in a Congress, or of some stupid boor in an obscure country parish. The electricity of universal sympathy, of action and reaction, pervades everything, the planets and the motes in the sunbeam. FAUST, with his types, or LUTHER, with his sermons, worked greater results than Alexander or Hannibal. A single thought sometimes suffices to overturn a dynasty. A silly song did more to unseat James the Second than the acquittal of the Bishops. Voltaire, Condorcet, and Rousseau uttered words that will ring, in change and revolutions, through all the ages.

Remember, that though life is short, Thought and the influences of what we do or say, are immortal; and that no calculus has yet pretended to ascertain the law of proportion between cause and effect. The hammer of an English blacksmith, smiting down an insolent official, led to a rebellion which came near being a revolution. The word well spoken, the deed fitly done, even by the feeblest or humblest, cannot help but have their effect. More or less, the effect is inevitable and eternal. The echoes of the greatest deeds may die away like the echoes of a cry among the cliffs, and what has been done seem to the human judgment to have been without result. The unconsidered act of the poorest of men may fire the train that leads to the subterranean mine, and an empire be rent by the explosion.

The power of a free people is often at the disposal of a single and seemingly an unimportant individual;—a terrible and truthful power; for such a people feel with one heart, and therefore can lift up their myriad arms for a single blow. And, again, there is no graduated scale for the measurement of the influences of different intellects upon the popular mind. Peter the Hermit held no office, yet what a work he wrought!

*   *   *   *   *   *

From the political point of view there is but a single principle,— the sovereignty of man over himself. This sovereignty of one's self over one's self is called LIBERTY. Where two or several of these sovereignties associate, the State begins. But in this association there is no abdication. Each sovereignty parts with a certain portion of itself to form the common right. That portion is the same for all. There is equal contribution by all to the joint sovereignty. This identity of concession which each makes to all, is EQUALITY. The common right is nothing more or less than the protection of all, pouring its rays on each. This protection of each by all, is FRATERNITY.

61

Liberty is the summit, Equality the base. Equality is not all vegetation on a level, a society of big spears of grass and stunted oaks, a neighborhood of jealousies, emasculating each other. It is civilly, all aptitudes having equal opportunity; politically, all votes having equal weight; religiously, all consciences having equal rights.

Equality has an organ;—gratuitous and obligatory instruction. We must begin with the right to the alphabet. The primary school *obligatory* upon all; the higher school *offered* to all. Such is the law. From the same school for all springs equal society. Instruction! Light! all comes from Light, and all returns to it.

We must learn the thoughts of the common people, if we would be wise and do any good work. We must look at men, not so much for what Fortune has given to them with her blind old eyes, as for the gifts Nature has brought in her lap, and for the use that has been made of them. We profess to be equal in a Church and in the Lodge: we shall be equal in the sight of God when He judges the earth. We may well sit on the pavement together here, in communion and conference, for the few brief moments that constitute life.

A Democratic Government undoubtedly has its defects, because it is made and administered by men, and not by the Wise Gods. It cannot be concise and sharp, like the despotic. When its ire is aroused it develops its latent strength, and the sturdiest rebel trembles. But its habitual domestic rule is tolerant, patient, and indecisive. Men are brought together, first to differ, and then to agree. Affirmation, negation, discussion, solution: these are the means of attaining truth. Often the enemy will be at the gates before the babble of the disturbers is drowned in the chorus of consent. In the Legislative office deliberation will often defeat decision. Liberty can play the fool like the Tyrants.

Refined society requires greater minuteness of regulation; and the steps of all advancing States are more and more to be picked among the old rubbish and the new materials. The difficulty lies in discovering the right path through the chaos of confusion. The adjustment of mutual rights and wrongs is also more difficult in democracies. We do not see and estimate the relative importance of objects so easily and clearly from the level or the waving land as from the elevation of a lone peak, towering above the plain ; for each looks through his own mist.

Abject dependence on constituents, also, is too common. It is as miserable a thing as abject dependence on a minister or the favorite of a Tyrant. It is rare to find a man who can speak out the simple truth that is in him, honestly and frankly, without fear, favor, or affection, either to Emperor or People.

Moreover, in assemblies of men, faith in each other is almost always wanting, unless a terrible pressure of calamity or danger from without produces cohesion. Hence the constructive power of such assemblies is generally deficient. The chief triumphs of modern days, in Europe, have been in pulling down and obliterating; not in building up. But Repeal is not Reform. Time must bring with him the Restorer and Rebuilder.

Speech, also, is grossly abused in Republics; and if the use of speech be glorious, its abuse is the most villainous of vices. Rhetoric, Plato says, is the art of ruling the minds of men. But in democracies it is too common to *hide* thought in words, to *overlay* it, to babble nonsense. The gleams and glitter of intellectual soap-and-water bubbles are mistaken for the rainbow-glories of genius. The worthless pyrites is continually mistaken for gold. Even intellect condescends to intellectual jugglery, balancing thoughts as a juggler balances pipes on his chin. In all Congresses we have the inexhaustible flow of babble, and Faction's clamorous knavery in discussion, until the divine power of speech, that privilege of man and great gift of God, is no better than the screech of parrots or the mimicry of monkeys. The mere talker, however fluent, is barren of deeds in the day of trial.

There are men voluble as women, and as well skilled in fencing with the tongue: prodigies of speech, misers in deeds. Too much talking, like too much thinking, destroys the power of action. In human nature, the thought is only made perfect by deed. Silence is the mother of both. The trumpeter is not the bravest of the brave. Steel and not brass wins the day. The great doer of great deeds is mostly slow and slovenly of speech. There are some men born and bred to betray. Patriotism is their trade, and their capital is speech. But no noble spirit can plead like Paul and be false to itself as Judas.

Imposture too commonly rules in republics; they seem to be ever in their minority; their guardians are self-appointed; and the unjust thrive better than the just. The Despot, like the night-lion roaring, drowns all the clamor of tongues at once, and

speech, the birthright of the free man, becomes the bauble of the
enslaved.

It is quite true that republics only occasionally, and as it were
accidentally, select their wisest, or even the less incapable among
the incapables, to govern them and legislate for them. If genius,
armed with learning and knowledge, will grasp the reins, the people
will reverence it; if it only modestly offers itself for office, it will
be smitten on the face, even when, in the straits of distress and
the agonies of calamity, it is indispensable to the salvation of the
State. Put it upon the track with the showy and superficial, the
conceited, the ignorant, and impudent, the trickster and charlatan,
and the result shall not be a moment doubtful. The verdicts of
Legislatures and the People are like the verdicts of juries,—sometimes right by accident.

Offices, it is true, are showered, like the rains of Heaven, upon
the just and the unjust. The Roman Augurs that used to laugh
in each other's faces at the simplicity of the vulgar, were also
tickled with their own guile; but no Augur is needed to lead the
people astray. They readily deceive themselves. Let a Republic
begin as it may, it will not be out of its minority before imbecility
will be promoted to high places; and shallow pretence, getting
itself puffed into notice, will invade all the sanctuaries. The most
unscrupulous partisanship will prevail, even in respect to judicial
trusts; and the most unjust appointments be constantly made,
although every improper promotion not merely confers one unde-
served favor, but may make a hundred honest cheeks smart with
injustice.

The country is stabbed in the front when those are brought into
the stalled seats who should slink into the dim gallery. Every
stamp of Honor, ill-clutched, is stolen from the Treasury of
Merit.

Yet the entrance into the public service, and the promotion in
it, affect both the rights of individuals and those of the nation.
Injustice in bestowing or withholding office ought to be so intolerable in democratic communities that the least trace of it should be
like the scent of Treason. It is not universally true that all citizens of equal character have an equal claim to knock at the door
of every public office and demand admittance. When any man
presents himself for service he has a right to aspire to the highest
body at once, if he can show his fitness for such a beginning,—that

he is fitter than the rest who offer themselves for the same post. The entry into it can only justly be made through the door of merit. And whenever any one aspires to and attains such high post, especially if by unfair and disreputable and indecent means, and is afterward found to be a signal failure, he should be at once beheaded. He is the worst among the public enemies.

When a man sufficiently reveals himself, all others should be proud to give him due precedence. When the power of promotion is abused in the grand passages of life, whether by People, Legislature, or Executive, the unjust decision recoils on the judge at once. That is not only a gross, but a willful shortness of sight, that cannot discover the deserving. If one will look hard, long, and honestly, he will not fail to discern merit, genius, and qualification; and the eyes and voice of the Press and Public should condemn and denounce injustice wherever she rears her horrid head.

"*The tools to the workmen!*" no other principle will save a Republic from destruction, either by civil war or the dry-rot. They tend to decay, do all we can to prevent it, like human bodies. If they try the experiment of governing themselves by their smallest, they slide downward to the unavoidable abyss with tenfold velocity; and there never has been a Republic that has not followed that fatal course.

But however palpable and gross the inherent defects of democratic governments, and fatal as the results finally and inevitably are, we need only glance at the reigns of Tiberius, Nero, and Caligula, of Heliogabalus and Caracalla, of Domitian and Commodus, to recognize that the difference between freedom and despotism is as wide as that between Heaven and Hell. The cruelty, baseness, and insanity of tyrants are incredible. Let him who complains of the fickle humors and inconstancy of a free people, read Pliny's character of Domitian. If the great man in a Republic cannot win office without descending to low arts and whining beggary and the judicious use of sneaking lies, let him remain in retirement, and use the pen. Tacitus and Juvenal held no office. Let History and Satire punish the pretender as they crucify the despot. The revenges of the intellect are terrible and just.

Let Masonry use the pen and the printing-press · in the free State against the Demagogue ; in the Despotism against the Tyrant. History offers examples and encouragement. All history, for four thousand years, being filled with violated rights and the

4

sufferings of the people, each period of history brings with it such protest as is possible to it. Under the Cæsars there was no insurrection, but there was a Juvenal. The arousing of indigna tion replaces the Gracchi. Under the Cæsars there is the exile of Syene; there is also the author of the Annals. As the Neros reign darkly they should be pictured so. Work with the graver only would be pale; into the grooves should be poured a concentrated prose that bites.

Despots are an aid to thinkers. Speech enchained is speech terrible. The writer doubles and triples his style, when silence is imposed by a master upon the people. There springs from this silence a certain mysterious fullness, which filters and freezes into brass in the thoughts. Compression in the history produces conciseness in the historian. The granitic solidity of some celebrated prose is only a condensation produced by the Tyrant. Tyranny constrains the writer to shortenings of diameter which are increases of strength. The Ciceronian period, hardly sufficient upon Verres, would lose its edge upon Caligula.

The Demagogue is the predecessor of the Despot. One springs from the other's loins. He who will basely fawn on those who have office to bestow, will betray like Iscariot, and prove a miserable and pitiable failure. Let the new Junius lash such men as they deserve, and History make them immortal in infamy; since their influences culminate in ruin. The Republic that employs and honors the shallow, the superficial, the base,

"who crouch

Unto the offal of an office promised"

at last weeps tears of blood for its fatal error. Of such supreme folly, the sure fruit is damnation. Let the nobility of every great heart, condensed into justice and truth, strike such creatures like a thunderbolt! If you can do no more, you can at least condemn by your vote, and ostracise by denunciation.

It is true that, as the Czars are absolute, they have it in their power to select the best for the public service. It is true that the beginner of a dynasty generally does so; and that when monarch-es are in their prime, pretence and shallowness do not thrive and prosper and get power, as they do in Republics. All do not gabble, in the Parliament of a kingdom, as in the Congress of a Democracy. The incapables do not go undetected there, *all* their lives.

But dinasties speedily decay and run out. At last they dwindle down into imbecility; and the dull or flippant Members of Congresses are at least the intellectual peers of the vast majority of kings. The great man, the Julius Cæsar, the Charlemagne, Cromwell, Napoleon, reigns of right. He is the wisest and the strongest The incapables and imbeciles succeed and are usurpers; and fear makes them cruel. After Julius came Caracalla and Galba ; after Charlemagne, the lunatic Charles the Sixth. So the Saracenic dynasty dwindled out; the Capets, the Stuarts, the Bour- bons; the last of these producing Bomba, the ape of Domitian.

    ＊   ＊   ＊   ＊   ＊   ＊

Man is by nature cruel, like the tigers. The barbarian, and the tool of the tyrant, and the civilized fanatic, enjoy the sufferings of others, as the children enjoy the contortions of maimed flies. Absolute Power, once in fear for the safety of its tenure, cannot but be cruel.

As to ability, dynasties invariably cease to possess any after a few lives. They become mere shams, governed by ministers, favor-ites, or courtesans, like those old Etruscan kings, slumbering for long ages in their golden royal robes, dissolving forever at the first breath of day. Let him who complains of the short-comings of democracy ask himself if he would prefer a Dubarry or a Pompa-dour, governing in the name of a Louis the Fifteen th, a Caligula making his horse a consul, a Domitian, "that most savage mon-ster," who sometimes drank the blood of relatives, sometimes em-ployed himself with slaughtering the most distinguished citizens. before whose gates fear and terror kept watch; A tyrant of fright- ful aspect, pride on his forehead, fire in his eye, constantly seeking darkness and secrecy, and only emerging from his solitude to make solitude? After all, in a free government, the Laws and the Con-stitution are above the Incapables, the Courts correct their legisla-tion, and posterity is the Grand Inquest that passes judgment on them. What is the exclusion of worth and intellect and knowl-edge from civil office compared with trials before Jeffries, tortures in the dark caverns of the Inquisition, Alva-butcheries in the Netherlands, the Eve of Saint Bartholomew, and the Sicilian Vespers?

    ＊   ＊   ＊   ＊   ＊   ＊

The Abbé Barruel in his *Memoirs for the History of* *Jaco*binism declares that Masonry in France gave, as its secret, the

words Equality and Liberty, leaving it for every honest and reli
gious Mason to explain them as would best suit his principles; but
retained the privilege of unveiling in the higher degrees the meaning of those words, as interpreted by the French Revolution. And
he also excepts English Masons from his anathemas, because in
England a Mason is a peaceable subject of the civil authorities,
no matter where he resides, engaging in no plots or conspiracies
against even the worst government. England, he says, disgusted
with an Equality and a Liberty, the consequences of which she
had felt in the struggles of her Lollards, Anabaptists, and Presby-
terians, had "purged her Masonry" from all explanations tending
to overturn empires; but there still remained adepts whom disor-
ganizing principles bound to the Ancient Mysteries.

Because true Masonry, unemasculated, bore the banners of Freedom and Equal Rights, and was in rebellion against temporal and
spiritual tyranny, its Lodges were proscribed in 1735, by an edict
of the States of Holland. In 1737, Louis XV. forbade them in
France. In 1738, Pope Clement XII. issued against them his
famous Bull of Excommunication, which was renewed by Benedict
XIV.; and in 1743 the Council of Berne also proscribed them.
The title of the Bull of Clement is, "The Condemnation of the
Society of Conventicles de Liberi Muratori, or of the Freemasons,
under the penalty of ipso facto excommunication, the absolution
from which is reserved to the Pope alone, except at the point
of death." And by it all bishops, ordinaries, and inquisitors
were empowered to punish Freemasons, "as vehemently sus-
pected of heresy," and to call in, if necessary, the help of the
secular arm; that is, to cause the civil authority to put them to
death.

   *   *   *   *   *   *

Also, false and slavish political theories end in brutalizing the
State. For example, adopt the theory that offices and employ-
ments in it are to be given us rewards for services rendered to
party, and they soon become the prey and spoil of faction, the
booty of the victory of faction;—and leprosy is in the flesh of the
State. The body of the commonwealth becomes a mass of corruption, like a living carcass rotten with syphilis. All unsound theories in the end develop themselves in one foul and loathsome disease
or other of the body politic. The State, like the man, must use
constant effort to stay in the parths of virtue and manliness. The

habit of electioneering and begging for office culminates in bribery *with* office, and corruption *in* office.

A chosen man has a visible trust from God, as plainly as if the commission were engrossed by the notary. A nation cannot renounce the executorship of the Divine decrees. As little can Masonry. It must labor to do its duty knowingly and wisely. We must remember that, in free States, as well as in despotisms, Injustice, the spouse of Oppression, is the fruitful parent of Deceit, Distrust, Hatred, Conspiracy, Treason, and Unfaithfulness. Even in assailing Tyranny we must have Truth and Reason as our chief weapons. We must march into that fight like the old Puritans, or into the battle with the abuses that spring up in free government, with the flaming sword in one hand, and the Oracles of God in the other.

The citizen who cannot accomplish well the smaller purposes of public life, cannot compass the larger. The vast power of endurance, forbearance, patience, and performance, of a free people, is only acquired by continual exercise of all the functions, like the healthful physical human vigor. If the individual citizens have it not, the State must be equally without it. It is of the essence of a free government, that the people should not only be concerned in making the laws, but also in their execution. No man ought to be more ready to obey and administer the law than he who has helped to make it. The business of government is carried on for the benefit of all, and every co-partner should give counsel and co-operation.

Remember also, as another shoal on which States are wrecked, that free States always tend toward the depositing of the citizens in strata, the creation of castes, the perpetuation of the *jus divinum* to office in families. The more democratic the State, the more sure this result. For, as free States advance in power, there is a strong tendency toward centralization, not from deliberate evil intention, but from the course of events and the indolence of human nature. The executive powers swell and enlarge to inordinate dimensions; and the Executive is always aggressive with respect to the nation. Offices of all kinds are multiplied to reward partisans; the brute force of the sewerage and lower strata of the mob obtains large representation, first in the lower offices, and at last in Senates; and Bureaucracy raises its bald head, bristling with pens, girded with spectacles, and bunched with ribbon. The art of Government becomes like a Craft, and its guilds tend to become exclusive, as those of the Middle Ages.

Political science may be much improved as a subject of *specialation*; but it should never be divorced from the actual national necessity. The science of governing men must always be practi-cal, rather than philosophical. There is not the same amonni of positive or uni versal truth here as in the abstract sciences; what is true in one country may be very false in another; what is untrue to-day may become true in another generation, and the truth of to-day be reversed by the judgment of to-morrow. To distinguish the casual from the enduring, to separate the unsuitable from the suitable, and to make progress even possible, are the proper ends of policy. But without actual knowledge and experience, and communion of labor, the dreams of the political doctors may be no better than those of the doctors of divinity. The reign of such a caste, with its mysteries, its myrmidons, and its corrupting influ-ence, may be as fatal as that of the despots. Thirty tyrants are thirty times worse than one.

Moreover, there is a strong temptation for the governing people to become as much slothful and sluggards as the weakest of absolute kings. Only give them the power to get rid, when caprice prompts them, of the great and wise men, and elect the little, and as to all the rest they will relapse into indolence and indifference. The central power, creation of the people, organized and cunning if not enlightened, is the perpetual tribunal set up by them for the redress of wrong and the rule of justice. It soon supplies itself with all the requisite machinery, and is ready and apt for all kinds of interference. The people may be a child all its life. The central power may not be able to suggest the best scientific solution of a problem ; but it has the easiest means of carrying an idea into effect. If the purpose to be attained is a large one, it requires a large comprehension ; it is proper for the action of the central power. If it be a small one, it may be thwarted by disagreement. The central power must step in as an arbitrator and prevent this. The people may be too averse to change, too slothful in their own business, unjust to a minority or a majority. The central power must take the reins when the people drop them.

France became centralized in its government, more by the apathy and ignorance of its people than by the tyranny of its kings. When the inmost parish-life is given up to the direct guardianship of the State, and the repair of the belfry of a country that requires a written order from the central power, a people is in its dotage. Men are thus nurtured in imbecility, from the dawn of social life. When the central government feeds part of the people, it prepares all to be slaves. When it directs parish and county affairs, they are slaves already. The next step is to regulate labor and its wages.

Nevertheless, whatever follies the free people may commit, even to the putting of the powers of legislation in the hands of the little competent and less honest, despair not of the final result. The terrible teacher, EXPERIENCE, writing his lessons on hearts desolated with calamity and wrung by agony, will make them wiser in time. Pretence and grimace and sordid beggary for votes will some day cease to avail. Have FAITH, and struggle on, against all evil influences and discouragements! FAITH is the Saviour and Redeemer of nations. When Christianity had grown weak, profitless, and powerless, the Arab Restorer and Iconoclast came, like a cleansing hurricane. When the battle of Damascus was about to be fought, the Christian bishop, at the early dawn, in his robes, at the head of his clergy, with the Cross once so triumphant raised in the air, came down to tho gates of the city, and laid open before the army the Testament of Christ. The Christian general, THOMAS, laid his hand on the book, and said, " *Oh God! IF our faith be true, aid us, and deliver us not into the hands of its enemies!*" But KHALED, "*the Sword of God,*" who had marched from victory to victory, exclaimed to his wearied soldiers, "*Let no man sleep! There will be rest enough in the bowers of Paradise; sweet will be the repose never more to be followed by labor.*" The faith of the Arab had become stronger than that of the Christian, and he conquered.

The Sword is also, in the Bible, an emblem of SPEECH, or of the utterance of thought. Thus, in that vision or apocalypse of the sublime exile of Patmos, a protest in the name of the ideal, over-whelming the real world, a tremendous satire uttered in the name of Religion and Liberty, and with its fiery reverberations smiting the throne of the Cæsars, a sharp two-edged sword comes out of the mouth of the Semblance of the Son of Man, encircled by the seven golden candlesticks, and holding in his right hand seven stars.

"The Lord," says Isaiah, "hath made my mouth like a sharp sword." "I have slain them," says *Hosea* "by the words

of my mouth." "The word of God," says the writer of the apos
tolic letter to the Hebrews, "is quick and powerful, and sharper
than any two-edged sword, piercing even to the dividing asunder
of soul and spirit." "The sword of the Spirit, which is the Word
of God," says Paul, writing to the Christians at Ephesus. "I will
fight against them with the sword of my mouth," it is said in the
Apocalypse, to the angel of the church at Pergamos.

      *   *   *   *   *   *

The spoken discourse may roll on strongly as the great tidal
wave; but, like the wave, it dies at last feebly on the sands. It is
heard by few, remembered by still fewer, and fades away, like an
echo in the mountains, leaving no token of power. It is nothing
to the living and coming generations of men. It was the *written*
human speech, that gave power and permanence to human thought.
It is this that makes the whole human history but one individual
life.

To write on the rock is to write on a solid parchment; but it
requires a pilgrimage to see it. There is but one copy, and Time
wears even that. To write on skins or papyrus was to give, as it
were, but one tardy edition, and the rich only could procure it.
The Chinese stereotyped not only the unchanging wisdom of old
sages, but also the passing events. The process tended to suffocate
thought, and to hinder progress; for there is continual wandering
in the wisest minds, and Truth writes her last words, not on clear
tablets, but on the scrawl that Error has made and often mended.

Printing made the movable letters prolific. Thenceforth the
orator spoke almost visibly to listening nations; and the author
wrote, like the Pope, his œcumenic decrees, *urbi et orbi*, and ordered them to be posted up in all the market-places; remaining,
if he chose, impervious to human sight. The doom of tyrannies
was thenceforth sealed. Satire and invective became potent as
armies. The unseen hands of the Juniuses could launch the thun-
derbolts, and make the ministers tremble. One whisper from this
giant fills the earth as easily as Demosthenes filled the Agora. It
will soon be heard at the antipodes as easily as in the next street.
It travels with the lightning under the oceans. It makes the
mass one man, speaks to it in the same common language, and
elicits a sure and single response. Speech passes into thought, and
thence promptly into act. A nation becomes truly one, with one
large heart and a single throbbing pulse. Men are invisibly presen

ent to each other, as if already spiritual beings; and the thinker who sits in an Alpine solitude, unknown to or forgotten by all the world, among the silent herds and hills, may flash his words to all the cities and over all the seas.

Select the thinkers to be Legislators; and avoid the gabblers. Wisdom is rarely loquacious. Weight and depth of thought are unfavorable to volubility. The shallow and superficial are generally voluble and often pass for eloquent. More words, less thought,—is the general rule. The man who endeavors to say something worth remembering in every sentence, becomes fastidious, and condenses like Tacitus. The vulgar love a more diffuse stream. The ornamentation that does not cover strength is the gewgaws of babble.

Neither is dialectic subtlety valuable to public men. The Christian faith has it, had it formerly more than now; a subtlety that might have entangled Plato, and which has rivalled in a fruitless fashion the mystic lore of Jewish Rabbis and Indian Sages. It is not this which converts the heathen. It is a vain task to balance the great thoughts of the earth, like hollow straws, on the finger-tips of disputation. It is not this kind of warfare which makes the Cross triumphant in the hearts of the unbelievers; but the actual power that lives in the Faith.

So there is a political scholasticism that is merely useless. The dexterities of subtle logic rarely stir the hearts of the people, or convince them. The true apostle of Liberty, Fraternity, and Equality makes it a matter of life and death. His combats are like those of Bossuet,—combats to the death. The true apostolic fire is like the lightning: it flashes conviction into the soul. The true word is verily a two-edged sword. Matters of government and political science can only be fairly dealt with by sound reason, and the logic of common sense: not the common sense of the ignorant, but of the wise. The acutest thinkers rarely succeed in becoming leaders of men. A watchword or a catchword is more potent with the people than logic, especially if this be the least metaphysical. When a political prophet arises, to stir the dreaming, stagnant nation, and hold back its feet from the irretrievable descent, to heave the land as with an earthquake, and shake the silly-shallow idols from their seats, his words will come straight from God's own mouth, and be thundered into the conscience. He will reason, teach, warn, and rule. The real " Sword of the Spirit' is keener than the brightest blade of Damascus. Such men rule a land, in the strength of justice, with wisdom and with power. Still, the men of dialectic subtlety often rule well, because in practice they forget their finely-spun theories, and use the trenchant logic of common sense. But when the great heart and large intellect are left to rust in private life, and small attorneys, brawlers in politics, and those who in the cities would be only the clerks of notaries, or practitioners in the disreputable courts, are made national Legislators, the country is in her dotage, even if the beard has not yet grown upon her chin.

In a free country, human speech must needs be free; and the State *must* listen to the maunderings of folly, and the screechings of its geese, and the brayings of its asses, as well as to the golden oracles of its wise and great men. Even the despotic old kings allowed their wise fools to say what they liked. The true alchemist will extract the lessons of wisdom from the babblings of folly. He will hear what a man has to say on any given subject, even if the speaker end only in proving himself prince of fools. Even a fool will sometimes hit the mark. There is some truth in all men who are not compelled to suppress their souls and speak other men's thoughts. The finger even of the idiot may point to the great highway.

A people, as well as the sages, must learn to forget. If it neither learns the new nor forgets the old, it is fated, even if it has been royal for thirty generations. To unlearn is to learn; and also it is sometimes needful to learn again the forgotten. The antics of fools make the current follies more palpable, as fashions are shown to be absurd by caricatures, which so lead to their extirpation. The buffoon and the zany are useful in their places. The ingenious artificer and craftsman, like Solomon, searches the earth for his materials, and transforms the misshapen matter into glorious workmanship. The world is conquered by the head even more than by the hands. Nor will any assembly talk forever. After a time, when it has listened long enough, it quietly puts the silly, the shallow, and the superficial to one side,—it thinks, and sets to work.

The human thought, especially in popular assemblies, runs in the most singularly crooked channels, harder to trace and follow than the blind currents of the ocean. No notion is so absurd that it may not find a place there. The master-workman must train these notions and vagaries with his two-handed hammer. They twist out of the way of the sword-thrusts; and are invulterable all over, even in the heel, against logic. The martel or mace, the battle-axe, the great double-edged two-handed sword must deal with follies; the rapier is no better against them than a wand, unless it be the rapier of ridicule.

The sword is also the symbol of *war* and of the *soldier*. Wars, like thunder-storms, are often necessary, to purify the stagnant atmosphere. War is not a demon, without remorse or reward. It restores the brotherhood in letters of fire. When men are seated in their pleasant places, sunken in ease and indolence, with Pretence and Incapacity and littleness usurping all the high places of State, war is the baptism of blood and fire, by which alone they can be renovated. It is the hurricane that brings the elemental equilibrium, the concord of Power and Wisdom. So long as these continue obstinately divorced, it will continue to chasten.

In the mutual appeal of nations to God, there is the acknowledgment of His might. It lights the beacons of Faith and Freedom, and heats the furnace through which the earnest and loyal pass to immortal glory. There is in war the doom of defeat, the quenchless sense of Duty, the stirring sense of Honor, the measureless solemn sacrifice of devotedness, and the incense of success. Even in the flame and smoke of battle, the Mason discovers his brother, and fulfills the sacred obligations of Fraternity.

Two, or the Duad, is the symbol of Antagonism; of Good and Evil, Light and Darkness. It is Cain and Abel, Eve and Lilith, Jachin and Boaz, Ormuzd and Ahriman, Osiris and Typhon.

Three, or the Triad, is most significantly expressed by the equilateral and the right-angled triangles. There are *three* principal colors or rays in the rainbow, which by intermixture make *seven*. The three are the *green*, the *yellow*, and the *red*. The Trinity of the Deity, in one mode or other, has been an article in all creeds. He creates, preserves, and destroys. He is the generative *power*, the productive *capacity*, and the *result*. The immaterial man, according to the Cabala, is composed of *vitality*, or *life*, the breath of life; of *soul* or *mind*, and *spirit*. Salt, sulphur, and mercury are the great symbols of the alchemists. To them man was body, soul, and spirit.

Four is expressed by the square, or four-sided right-angled

figure. Out of the symbolic Garden of Eden flowed a river, divid
ing into *four* streams,—PISON, which flows around the land of
gold, or light; GIHON, which flows around the land of Ethiopia
or Darkness; HIDDEKEL, running eastward to Assyria; and the
EUPHRATES. Zechariah saw *four* chariots coming out from between two mountains of bronze, in the first of which were *red*
horses; in the second, *black;* in the third, *white;* and in the
fourth, *grizzled:* "and these were the four winds of the heavens,
that go forth from standing before the Lord of all the earth."
Ezekiel saw the *four* living creatures, each with *four* faces and
four wings, the faces of a *man* and a *lion*, an *ox* and an *eagle;*
and the *four* wheels going upon their *four* sides; and Saint John
beheld the *four* beasts, full of eyes before and behind, the LION,
the young Ox, the MAN, and the flying EAGLE. *Four* was the
signature of the Earth. Therefore, in the 148th Psalm, of those
who must praise the Lord on the land, there are *four* times *four*,
and *four* in particular of living creatures. Visible nature is de-
scribed as the *four* quarters of the world, and the *four* corners of
the earth. "There are *four*," says the old Jewish saying, "which
take the first place in this world; *man*, among the creatures;
the *eagle* among birds; the *ox* among cattle; and the *lion*
among wild beasts." Daniel saw *four* great beasts come up from
the sea.

FIVE is the Duad added to the Triad. It is expressed by the
five-pointed or blazing star, the mysterious Pentalpha of Pythagoras. It is indissolubly connected with the number *seven*. Christ
fed his disciples and the multitude with *five* loaves and *two* fishes,
and of the fragments there remained *twelve*, that is, *five* and *seven*,
baskets full. Again he fed them with *seven* loaves and a few little
fishes, and there remained *seven* baskets full. The *five* apparently
small planets, Mercury, Venus, Mars, Jupiter, and Saturn, with the
two greater ones, the Sun and Moon, constituted the *seven* celestial
spheres.

SEVEN was the peculiarly sacred number. There were *seven*
planets and spheres, presided over by *seven* archangels. There were
seven colors in the rainbow; and the Phœnician Deity was called
the HEPTAKTIS, or God of *seven* rays: *seven* days of the week;
and *seven* and *five* made the number of months, tribes, and apostles. Zechariah saw a golden candlestick, with *seven* lamps and
seven pipes to the lamps, and an olive-tree on each side. "Since,"

he says, "the *seven* eyes of the Lord shall rejoice, and shall see the plummet in the hand of Zerubbabel." John, in the Apocalypse, writes *seven* epistles to the *seven* churches. In the *seven* epistles there are *twelve* promises. What is said of the churches is *praise* or blame, is completed in the number *three*. The refrain, "*who has ears to hear*," etc., has *ten* words, divided by *three* and *seven*, and the *seven* by *three* and *four ;* and the *seven* epistles are also so divided. In the seals, trumpets, and vials, also, of this symbolic vision, the *seven* are divided by *four* and *three*. He who sends his message to Ephesus, "holds the *seven* stars in his right hand, and walks amid the *seven* golden lamps."

In *six* days, or periods, God created the universe, and paused on the *seventh* day. Of clean beasts, Noah was directed to take by *sevens* into the ark ; and of fowls by *sevens ;* because in *seven* days the rain was to commence. On the *seven*teenth day of the month, the rain began ; on the *seven*teenth day of the *seventh* month, the ark rested on Ararat. When the dove returned, Noah waited *seven* days before he sent her forth again ; and again *seven*, after she returned with the olive-leaf. Enoch was the *seventh* patriarch, Adam included, and Lamech lived 777 years.

There were *seven* lamps in the great candlestick of the Tabernacle and Temple, representing the *seven* planets. *Seven* times Moses sprinkled the anointing oil upon the altar. The days of consecration of Aaron and his sons were *seven* in number. A woman was unclean *seven* days after child-birth ; one infected with leprosy was shut up *seven* days ; *seven* times the leper was sprinkled with the blood of a slain bird ; and *seven* days afterward he must remain abroad out of his tent. *Seven* times, in purifying the leper, the priest was to sprinkle the consecrated oil ; and *seven* times to sprinkle with the blood of the sacrificed bird the house to be purified. *Seven* times the blood of the slain bullock was sprinkled on the mercy-seat ; and *seven* times on the altar. The *seventh* year was a Sabbath of rest ; and at the end of *seven* times *seven* years came the great year of jubilee. *Seven* days the people ate unleavened bread, in the month of Abib. *Seven* weeks were counted from the time of first putting the sickle to the wheat. The Feast of the Tabernacles lasted *seven* days.

Israel was in the land of Midian *seven* years, before Gideon delivered them. The bullock sacrificed by him was *seven* years old. Samson told Delilah to bind him with *seven* green withes ; and she wove the *seven* locks of his head, and afterward shaved them off. Balaam told Barak to build for him *seven* altars. Jacob served *seven* years for Leah and *seven* for Rachel. Job had *seven* sons and *three* daughters, making the perfect number *ten*. He had also *seven* thousand sheep and *three* thousand camels. His friends sat down with him *seven* days and *seven* nights. His friends were ordered to sacrifice *seven* bullocks and *seven* rams; and again, at the end, he had *seven* sons and *three* daughters, and twice *seven* thousand sheep, and lived an hundred and forty, or twice *seven* times *ten* years. Pharaoh saw in his dream *seven* fat and *seven* lean kine, *seven* good ears and *seven* blasted ears of wheat; and there were *seven* years of plenty, and *seven* of famine. Jericho fell, when *seven* priests, with *seven* trumpets, made the circuit of the city on *seven* successive days; once each day for six days, and *seven* times on the seventh. "The *seven* eyes of the Lord," says Zechariah, "run to and fro through the whole earth." Solomon was *seven* years in building the Temple. *Seven* angels, in the Apocalypse, pour out *seven* plagues, from *seven* vials of wrath. The scarlet-colored beast, on which the woman sits in the wilderness, has *seven* heads and *ten* horns. So also has the beast that rises up out of the sea. *Seven* thunders uttered their voices. *Seven* angels sounded *seven* trumpets. *Seven* lamps of fire, the *seven* spirits of God, burned before the throne; and the Lamb that was slain had *seven* horns and *seven* eyes.

EIGHT is the first cube, that of *two*. NINE is the square of *three*, and represented by the triple triangle.

TEN includes all the other numbers. It is especially *seven* and *three;* and is called the number of perfection. Pythagoras represented it by the TETRACTYS, which had many mystic meanings. This symbol is sometimes composed of dots or points, sometimes of commas or yōds, and in the Cabala, of the letters of the name of Deity. It is thus arranged:

The Patriarchs from Adam to Noah, inclusive, are *ten* in number, and the same number is that of the Commandments.

TWELVE is the number of the lines of equal length that form a cube. It is the number of the months, the tribes, and the apostles; of the oxen under the Brazen Sea, of the stones on the breast plate of the high priest.

•   •   •   •   •   •

•   •   *   *   *   *

III.
THE MASTER.

*   *   *   *   *   *

To understand literally the symbols and allegories of Oriental books as to ante-historical matters, is willfully to close our eyes against the Light. To translate the symbols into the trivial·and commonplace, is the blundering of mediocrity.

All religious expression is symbolism; since we can *describe* only what we *see*, and the true objects of religion are THE SEEN. The earliest instruments of education were symbols; and they and all other religious forms differed and still differ according to external circumstances and imagery, and according to differences of knowledge and mental cultivation. All language is symbolic, so far as it is applied to mental and spiritual phenomena and action. All *words* have, primarily, a *material* sense, howsoever they may afterward get, for the ignorant, a spiritual *non*-sense. To "retract," for example, is to *draw back*, and when applied to a *statement*, is symbolic, as much so as a picture of an arm drawn back, to express the same thing, would be. The very word "*spirit*" means "*breath*," from the Latin verb *spiro, breathe.*

To present a visible symbol to the eye of another, is not neces sarily to inform him of the meaning which that symbol has to you. Hence the philosopher soon superadded to the symbols explanations addressed to the ear, susceptible of more precision, but less effective and impressive than the painted or sculptured forms which he endeavored to explain. Out of these explanations grew by degrees a variety of narrations, whose true object and meaning were gradually forgotten, or lost in contradictions and incongruities. And when these were abandoned, and Philosophy resorted to definitions and formulas, its language was but a more complicated symbolism, attempting in the dark to grapple with and picture ideas impossible to be expressed. For as with the visible symbol, so with the word: to utter it to you does not inform you of the *exact* meaning which it has to *me ;* and thus religion and philosophy became to a great extent disputes as to the meaning

86

of words. The most abstract expression for DEITY, which language can supply, is but a *sign* or *symbol* for an object beyond our comprehension, and not more truthful and adequate than the images of OSIRIS and VISHNU, or their names, except as being less sensuous and explicit. We avoid sensuousness, only by resorting to simple negation. We come at last to define spirit by saying that it is not matter. Spirit is—spirit.

A single example of the symbolism of *words* will indicate to you one branch of Masonic study. We find in the English Rite this phrase : "I will always *hail*, ever conceal, and never reveal;" and in the Catechism, these:

Q∴ "*I hail.*"

A∴ "*I conceal;*"

and ignorance, misunderstanding the word "*hail*," has interpolated the phrase, "From whence do you *hail?*"

But the word is really "*hele*," from the Anglo-Saxon verb Delan, *helan*, to *cover, hide*, or *conceal*. And this word is rendered by the Latin verb *tegere*, to *cover* or *roof over*. "That ye fro me no thynge woll hele," says Gower. "They *hele* fro me no priuyte," says the Romaunt of the Rose. "To *heal* a house," is a common phrase in Sussex; and in the west of England, he that covers a house with slates is called a *Healer*. Wherefore, to "*heal*" means the same thing as to "*tile*,"—itself symbolic, as meaning, primarily, to *cover* a house with *tiles*,—and means to *cover, hide*, or *conceal*. Thus language too is symbolism, and words are as much misunderstood and misused as more material symbols are.

Symbolism tended continually to become more complicated; and all the powers of Heaven were reproduced on earth, until a web of fiction and allegory was woven, partly by art and partly by the ignorance of error, which the wit of man, with his limited means of explanation, will never unravel. Even the Hebrew Theism became involved in symbolism and image-worship, borrowed probably from an older creed and remote regions of Asia,—the worship of the Great Semitic Nature-God AL or EL : and its symbolical representations of JEHOVAH Himself were not even confined to poetical or illustrative language. The priests were monotheists: the people idolaters.

There are dangers inseparable from symbolism, which afford an impressive lesson in regard to the similar risks attendant on the use of language. The imagination, called in to assist the reason

5

64 MORALS AND DOGMA.

usurps its place or leaves its ally helplessly entangled in its web
Names which stand for things are confounded with them; the
means are mistaken for the end; the instrument of interpretation
for the object; and thus symbols come to usurp an independent
character as truths and persons. Though perhaps a necessary
path, they were a dangerous one by which to approach the Deity;
in which many, says PLUTARCH, "mistaking the sign for the thing
signified, fell into a ridiculous superstition; while others, in avoid-
ing one extreme, plunged into the no less hideous gulf of irreligion
and impiety."

It is through the mysteries, CICERO says, that we have learned
the first principles of life; wherefore the term "initiation" is used
with good reason; and they not only teach us to live more happily
and agreeably, but they soften the pains of death by the hope of a
better life hereafter.

The mysteries were a Sacred Drama. exhibiting some legend significant of nature's changes, of the visible universe in which the
Divinity is revealed, and whose import was in many respects as
open to the Pagan as to the Christian. Nature is the great Teacher
of man; for it is the Revelation of God. It neither dogmatizes nor
attempts to tyrannize by compelling to a particular creed or special interpretation. It presents its symbols to us, and adds nothing
by way of explanation. It is the text without the commentary;
and, as we well know, it is chiefly the commentary and gloss that
lead to error and heresy and persecution. The earliest instructors
of mankind not only adopted the lessons of Nature, but as far as
possible adhered to her method of imparting them. In the mysteries, beyond the current traditions or sacred and enigmatic recitals
of the Temples, few explanations were given to the spectators,
who were left, as in the school of nature, to make inferences for
themselves. No other method could have suited every degree of
cultivation and capacity. To employ nature's universal symbolism
instead of the technicalities of language, rewards the humblest in-
quirer, and discloses its secrets to every one in proportion to his
preparatory training and his power to comprehend them. If their
philosophical meaning was above the comprehension of some, their
moral and political meanings are within the reach of all.

These mystic shows and performances were not the reading of
a lecture, but the opening of a problem. Requiring research, they
were calculated to arouse the dormant intellect. They implied no

88

hostility to Philosophy, because Philosophy is the great expounder of symbolism; although its ancient interpretations were often ill-founded and incorrect. The alteration from symbol to dogma is fatal to beauty of expression, and leads to intolerance and assumed infallibility.

* * * * * *

If, in teaching the great doctrine of the divine nature of the Soul, and in striving to explain its longings after immortality, and in proving its superiority over the souls of the animals, which have no aspirations Heavenward, the ancients struggled in vain to express the *nature* of the soul, by comparing it to FIRE and LIGHT, it will be well for us to consider whether, with all our boasted knowledge, we have any better or clearer idea of its nature, and whether we have not despairingly taken refuge in having none at all. And if they erred as to its original place of abode, and understood literally the mode and path of its descent, these were but the accessories of the great Truth, and probably, to the initiates, mere allegories, designed to make the idea more palpable and impressive to the mind.

They are at least no more fit to be smiled at by the self-conceit of a vain ignorance, the wealth of whose knowledge consists solely in words, than the *bosom* of Abraham, as a home for the *spirits* of the just dead; the gulf of actual fire, for the eternal torture of *spirits ;* and the City of the New Jerusalem, with its walls of jasper and its edifices of pure gold like clear glass, its foundations of precious stones, and its gates each of a single pearl. "I knew a man," says PAUL, "caught up to the third Heaven; ... that he was caught up into Paradise, and heard ineffable words, which it is not possible for a man to utter." And nowhere is the antagonism and conflict between the spirit and body more frequently and forcibly insisted on than in the writings of this apostle, nowhere the Divine nature of the soul more strongly asserted. "With the mind," he says, "I serve the law of God ; but with the flesh the law of sin. ... As many as are led by the Spirit of God, are the sons of God. ... The earnest expectation of the created waits for the manifestation of the sons of God. ... The created shall be delivered from the bondage of corruption, of the flesh liable to decay, into the glorious liberty of the children of God."

* * * * * *

Two forms of government are favorable to the prevalence of

falsehood and deceit. Under a Despotism, men are false, treachu-
ous, and deceitful through fear, like slaves dreading the lash.
Under a Democracy they are so as a means of attaining popularity
and office, and because of the greed for wealth. Experience will
probably prove that these odious and detestable vices will grow
most rankly and spread most rapidly in a Republic. When office
and wealth become the gods of a people, and the most unworthy
and unfit most aspire to the former, and fraud becomes the highway to the latter, the land will reek with falsehood and sweat lies
and chicane. When the offices are open to all, merit and stern integrity and the dignity of unsullied honor will attain them only
rarely and by accident. To be able to serve the country well, will
cease to be a reason why the great and wise and learned should be
selected to render service. Other qualifications, less honorable,
will be more available. To adapt one's opinions to the popular
humor ; to defend, apologize for, and justify the popular follies ; to
advocate the expedient and the plausible ; to caress, cajole, and flatter the elector ; to beg like a spaniel for his vote, even if he be a
negro three removes from barbarism ; to profess friendship for a
competitor and stab him by inuendo ; to set on foot that which at
third hand shall become a lie, being cousin-german to it when uttered, and yet capable of being explained away,—who is there that
has not seen these low arts and base appliances put in practice, and
becoming general, until success cannot be surely had by any more
honorable means?—the result being a State ruled and ruined by
ignorant and shallow mediocrity, pert self-conceit, the greenness
of unripe intellect, vain of a school-boy's smattering of knowledge.

The faithless and the false in public and in political life, will be
faithless and false in private. The jockey in politics, like the
jockey on the race-course, is rotten from skin to core. Everywhere he will see first to his own interests, and whoso leans on him
will be pierced with a broken reed. His ambition is ignoble, like
himself; and therefore he will seek to attain office by ignoble
means, as he will seek to attain any other coveted object,—land,
money, or reputation.

At length, office and honor are divorced. The place that the
small and shallow, the knave or the trickster, is deemed competent
and fit to fill, ceases to be worthy the ambition of the great and
capable; or if not, these shrink from a contest, the weapons to be
used wherein are unfit for a gentleman to handle. Then the habits

ot unprincipled advocates in law courts are naturalized in Senates, and pettifoggers wrangle there, when the fate of the nation and the lives of millions are at stake. States are even begotten by villainy and brought forth by fraud, and rascalities are justified by legislators claiming to be honorable. Then contested elections are decided by perjured votes or party considerations; and all the practices of the worst times of corruption are revived and exaggerated in Republics.

It is strange that reverence for truth, that manliness and genuine loyalty, and scorn of littleness and unfair advantage, and genuine faith and godliness and large-heartedness should diminish, among statesmen and people, as civilization advances, and freedom becomes more general, and universal suffrage implies universal worth and fitness! In the age of Elizabeth, without universal suffrage, or Societies for the Diffusion of Useful Knowledge, or popular lecturers, or Lycæa, the statesman, the merchant, the burgher, the sailor, were all alike heroic, fearing God only, and man not at all. Let but a hundred or two years elapse, and in a Monarchy or Republic of the same race, nothing is *less* heroic than the merchant, the shrewd speculator, the office-seeker, fearing man only, and God not at all. Reverence for greatness dies out, and is succeeded by base envy of greatness. Every man is in the way of many, either in the path to popularity or wealth. There is a general feeling of satisfaction when a great statesman is displaced, or a general, who has been for his brief hour the popular idol, is unfortunate and sinks from his high estate. It becomes a misfortune, if not a crime, to be above the popular level.

We should naturally suppose that a nation in distress would take counsel with the wisest of its sons. But, on the contrary, great men seem never so scarce as when they are most needed, and small men never so bold to insist on infesting place, as when mediocrity and incapable pretence and sophomoric greenness, and showy and sprightly incompetency are most dangerous. When France was in the extremity of revolutionary agony, she was governed by an assembly of provincial pettifoggers, and Robespierre, Marat, and Couthon ruled in the place of Mirabeau, Vergniaud, and Carnot. England was governed by the Rump Parliament, after she had beheaded her king. Cromwell extinguished one body, and Napoleon the other.

Fraud, falsehood, trickery, and deceit in national affairs, are the

signs of decadence in States and precede convulsions or paralysia
To bully the weak and crouch to the strong, is the policy of nations governed by small mediocrity. The tricks of the canvass for
office are re-enacted in Senates. The Executive becomes the dis-
penser of patronage, chiefly to the most unworthy; and men are
bribed with offices instead of money, to the greater ruin of the
Commonwealth. The Divine in human nature disappears, and interest, greed, and selfishness take its place. That is a sad and true
allegory which represents the companions of Ulysses changed by
the enchantments of Circe into swine.

*   *   *   *   *   *

"Ye cannot," said the Great Teacher, "serve God and Mammon." When the thirst for wealth becomes general, it will be
sought for as well dishonestly as honestly; by frauds and overreachings, by the knaveries of trade, the heartlessness of greedy
speculation, by gambling in stocks and commodities that soon de-
moralizes a whole community. Men will speculate upon the needs
of their neighbors and the distresses of their country. Bubbles
that, bursting, impoverish multitudes, will be blown up by cunning knavery, with stupid credulity as its assistant and instrument Huge bankruptcies, that startle a country like the earthquakes, and are more fatal, fraudulent assignments, engulfment of
the savings of the poor, expansions and collapses of the currency,
the crash of banks, the depreciation of Government securities,
prey on the savings of self-denial, and trouble with their depreda-
tions the first nourishment of infancy and the last sands of life,
and fill with inmates the churchyards and lunatic asylums. But
the sharper and speculator thrives and fattens. If his country is
fighting by a levy en masse for her very existence, he aids her by
depreciating her paper, so that he may accumulate fabulous
amounts with little outlay. If his neighbor is distressed, he buys
his property for a song. If he administers upon an estate, it turns
out insolvent, and the orphans are paupers. If his bank explodes,
he is found to have taken care of himself in time. Society wor-
ships its paper-and-credit kings, as the old Hindûs and Egyptians
worshipped their worthless idols, and often the most obsequiously
when in actual solid wealth they are the veriest paupers. No
wonder men think there ought to be another world, in which the
injustices of this may be atoned for, when they see the friends of
ruined families begging the wealthy sharpers to give alms to pre

rent the orphaned victims from starving, until they may find
ways of supporting themselves.

    *   *   *   *   *   *

States are chiefly avaricious of commerce and of territory. The
latter leads to the violation of treaties, encroachments upon feeble
neighbors, and rapacity toward their wards whose lands are coveted. Republics are, in this, as rapacious and unprincipled as
Despots, never learning from history that inordinate expansion by
rapine and fraud has its inevitable consequences in dismemberment or subjugation. When a Republic begins to plunder its
neighbors, the words of doom are already written on its walls.
There is a judgment already pronounced of God, upon whatever is
unrighteous in the conduct of national affairs. When civil war
tears the vitals of a Republic, let it look back and see if it has not
been guilty of injustices; and if it has, let it humble itself in the
dust!

When a nation becomes possessed with a spirit of commercial
greed, beyond those just and fair limits set by a due regard to a
moderate and reasonable degree of general and individual prosperity, it is a nation possessed by the devil of commercial avarice, a
passion as ignoble and demoralizing as avarice in the individual;
and as this sordid passion is baser and more unscrupulous than
ambition, so it is more hateful, and at last makes the infected na
tion be regarded as the enemy of the human race. To grasp at
the lion's share of commerce, has always at last proven the ruin of
States, because it invariably leads to injustices that make a State
detestable; to a selfishness and crooked policy that forbid other
nations to be the friends of a State that cares only for itself.

Commercial avarice in India was the parent of more atrocities
and greater rapacity, and cost more human lives, than the nobler
ambition for extended empire of Consular Rome. The nation
that grasps at the commerce of the world cannot but become
selfish, calculating, dead to the noblest impulses and sympathies
which ought to actuate States. It will submit to insults that
wound its honor, rather than endanger its commercial interests by
war; while, to subserve those interests, it will wage unjust war,
on false or frivolous pretexts, its free people cheerfully allying
themselves with despots to crush a commercial rival that has
dared exile its kings and elect its own ruler.

Thus the cold calculations of a sordid self-interest, in nations

commercially avaricious, always at last displace the sentiments and
lofty impulses of Honor and Generosity by which they rose to
greatness; which made Elizabeth and Cromwell alike the pro-
tectors of Protestants beyond the four seas of England, against
crowned Tyranny and mitred Persecution; and, if they had
lasted, would have forbidden alliances with Czars and Autocrats
and Bourbons to re-enthrone the Tyrannies of Incapacity, and
arm the Inquisition anew with its instruments of torture. The
soul of the avaricious nation petrifies, like the soul of the individual who makes gold his god. The Despot will occasionally act
upon noble and generous impulses, and help the weak against the
strong, the right against the wrong. But commercial avarice is
essentially egotistic, grasping, faithless, overreaching, crafty, cold,
ungenerous, selfish, and calculating, controlled by considerations
of self-interest alone. Heartless and merciless, it has no sentiments of pity, sympathy, or honor, to make it pause in its remorse-
less career; and it crushes down all that is of impediment in its
way, as its keels of commerce crush under them the murmuring
and unheeded waves.

A war for a great principle ennobles a nation. A war for commercial supremacy, upon some shallow pretext, is despicable, and
more than aught else demonstrates to what immeasurable depths
of baseness men and nations can descend. Commercial greed values the lives of men no more than it values the lives of ants. The
slave-trade is as acceptable to a people enthralled by that greed, as
the trade in ivory or spices, if the profits are as large. It will by-
and-by endeavor to compound with God and quiet its own conscience, by compelling those to whom it sold the slaves it bought
or stole, to set them free, and slaughtering them by hecatombs if
they refuse to obey the edicts of its philanthropy.

Justice in no wise consists in meting out to another that exact
measure of reward or punishment which we think and decree his
merit, or what we call his crime, which is more often merely his
error, deserves. The justice of the father is not incompatible
with forgiveness by him of the errors and offences of his child.
The Infinite Justice of God does not consist in meting out exact
measures of punishment for human frailties and sins. We are too
apt to erect our own little and narrow notions of what is right and
just, into the law of justice, and to insist that God shall adopt
that as His law; to measure off something with our own little

tape-line, and call it God's law of justice. Continually we seek to ennoble our own ignoble love of revenge and retaliation, by misnaming it justice.

Nor does justice consist in strictly governing our conduct toward other men by the rigid rules of legal right. If there were a community anywhere, in which all stood upon the strictness of this rule, there should be written over its gates, as a warning to the unfortunates desiring admission to that inhospitable realm, the words which DANTE says are written over the great gate of Hell: "LET THOSE WHO ENTER HERE LEAVE HOPE BEHIND!" It is not just to pay the laborer in field or factory or workshop his current wages and no more, the lowest market-value of his labor, for so long only as we need that labor and he is able to work; for when sickness or old age overtakes him, that is to leave him and his family to starve; and God will curse with calamity the people in which the children of the laborer out of work eat the boiled grass of the field, and mothers strangle their children, that they may buy food for themselves with the charitable pittance given for burial expenses. The rules of what is ordinarily termed "*Justice*," may be punctiliously observed among the fallen spirits that are the aristocracy of Hell.

* * * * * *

Justice, divorced from sympathy, is selfish indifference, not in the least more laudable than misanthropic isolation. There is sympathy even among the hair-like oscillatorias, a tribe of simple plants, armies of which may be discovered, with the aid of the microscope, in the tiniest bit of scum from a stagnant pool. For these will place themselves, as if it were by agreement, in separate companies, on the side of a vessel containing them, and seem marching upward in rows; and when a swarm grows weary of its situation, and has a mind to change its quarters, each army holds on its way without confusion or intermixture, proceeding with great regularity and order, as if under the directions of wise leaders. The ants and bees give each other mutual assistance, beyond what is required by that which human creatures are apt to regard as the strict law of justice.

Surely we need but reflect a little, to be convinced that the individual man is but a fraction of the unit of society, and that he is indissolubly connected with the rest of his race. Not only the actions, but the will and thoughts of other men make or mar his fortunes, control his destinies, are unto him life or death, dishonor or honor. The epidemics, physical and moral, contagious and infectious, public opinion, popular delusions, enthusiasms, and the other great electric phenomena and currents, moral and intellectual, prove the universal sympathy. The vote of a single and obscure man, the utterance of self-will, ignorance, conceit, or spite, deciding an election and placing Folly or Incapacity or Baseness in a Senate, involves the country in war, sweeps away our fortunes, slaughters our sons, renders the labors of a life unavailing, and pushes us, helpless, with all our intellect, to resist, into the grave.

These considerations ought to teach us that justice to others and to ourselves is the same; that we cannot define our duties by mathematical lines ruled by the square, but must fill with them the great circle traced by the compasses; that the circle of humanity is the limit, and we are but the point in its centre, the drops in the great Atlantic, the atom or particle, bound by a mysterious law of attraction which we term sympathy to every other atom in the mass; that the physical and moral welfare of others cannot be indifferent to us; that we have a direct and immediate interest in the public morality and popular intelligence, in the well-being and physical comfort of the people at large. The ignorance of the people, their pauperism and destitution, and consequent degradation, their brutalization and demoralization, are all diseases; and we cannot rise high enough above the people, nor shut ourselves up from them enough, to escape the miasmatic contagion and the great magnetic currents.

Justice is peculiarly indispensable to nations. The unjust State is doomed of God to calamity and ruin. This is the teaching of the Eternal Wisdom and of history. "Righteousness exalteth a nation; but wrong is a reproach to nations." "The Throne is established by Righteousness. Let the lips of the Ruler pronounce the sentence that is Divine; and his mouth do no wrong in judgment!" The nation that adds province to province by fraud and violence, that encroaches on the weak and plunders its wards, and violates its treaties and the obligation of its contracts, and for the law of honor and fair-dealing substitutes the exigencies of greed and the base precepts of policy and craft and the ignoble tenets of expediency, is predestined to destruction; for here, as with the individual, the consequences of wrong are inevitable and eternal.

A sentence is written against all that is unjust, written by God

in the nature of man and in the nature of the universe, because it
is in the nature of the Infinite God. No wrong is really successful
The gain of injustice is a loss; its pleasure, suffering. Iniquity
often seems to prosper, but its success is its defeat and shame. If
its consequences pass by the doer, they fall upon and crush his
children. It is a philosophical, physical, and moral truth, in the
form of a threat, that God visits the iniquity of the fathers upon
the children, to the third and fourth generation of those who vio-
late His laws. After a long while, the day of reckoning always
comes, to nation as to individual; and always the knave deceives
himself, and proves a failure.

Hypocrisy is the homage that vice and wrong pay to virtue and
justice. It is Satan attempting to clothe himself in the angelic
vesture of Light. It is equally detestable in morals, politics, and
religion; in the man and in the nation. To do injustice under the
pretence of equity and fairness; to reprove vice in public and commit it in private; to pretend to charitable opinion and censoriously
condemn ; to profess the principles of Masonic beneficence, and close
the ear to the wail of distress and the cry of suffering ; to eulogise
the intelligence of the people, and plot to deceive and betray them
by means of their ignorance and simplicity; to prate of purity,
and peculate; of honor, and basely abandon a sinking cause; of
disinterestedness, and sell one's vote for place and power, are hypocrisies as common as they are infamous and disgraceful. To steal the
livery of the Court of God to serve the Devil withal; to pretend to
believe in a God of mercy and a Redeemer of love, and persecute
those of a different faith ; to devour widows' houses, and for a pretence make long prayers; to preach continence, and wallow in lust;
to inculcate humility, and in pride surpass Lucifer; to pay tithe,
and omit the weightier matters of the law, judgment, mercy, and
faith; to strain at a gnat, and swallow a camel; to make clean
the outside of the cup and platter, keeping them full within of ex-
tortion and excess; to appear outwardly righteous unto men, but
within be full of hypocrisy and iniquity, is indeed to be like unto
whited sepulchres, which appear beautiful outward, but are within
full of bones of the dead and of all uncleanness.

The Republic cloaks its ambition with the pretence of a desire
and duty to "extend the area of fieedom," and claims it as its
"manifest destiny" to annex other Republics or the States or
Provinces of others to itself, by open violence, or under obsolete,

empty, and fraudulent titles. The Empire founded by a successfu.
soldier, claims its ancient or natural boundaries, and makes necessity and its safety the plea for open robbery. The great Merchant
Nation, gaining foothold in the Orient, finds a continual necessity
for extending its dominion by arms, and subjugates India. The
great Royalties and Despotisms, without a plea, partition among
themselves a Kingdom, dismember Poland, and prepare to wrangl(
over the dominions of the Crescent. To maintain the balance of
power is a plea for the obliteration of States. Carthage, Genoa,
and Venice, commercial Cities only, must acquire territory by force
or fraud, and become States. Alexander marches to the Indus;
Tamerlane seeks universal empire; the Saracens conquer Spain
and threaten Vienna.

The thirst for power is never satisfied. It is insatiable. Neither
men nor nations ever have power enough. When Rome was the
mistress of the world, the Emperors caused themselves to be worshipped as gods. The Church of Rome claimed despotism over
the soul, and over the whole life from the cradle to the grave. It
gave and sold absolutions for past and future sins. It claimed to
be infallible in matters of faith. It decimated Europe to purge it
of heretics. It decimated America to convert the Mexicans and
Peruvians. It gave and took away thrones; and by excommunication and interdict closed the gates of Paradise against Nations.
Spain, haughty with its dominion over the Indies, endeavored to
crush out Protestantism in the Netherlands, while Philip the
Second married the Queen of England, and the pair sought to win
that kingdom back to its allegiance to the Papal throne. Afterward Spain attempted to conquer it with her "invincible" Ar-
mada. Napoleon set his relatives and captains on thrones, and
parcelled among them half of Europe. The Czar rules over an
empire more gigantic than Rome. The history of all is or will be
the same,—acquisition, dismemberment, ruin. There is a judgment of God against all that is unjust.

To seek to subjugate the *will* of others and take the *soul* cap-
tive, because it is the exercise of the highest power, seems to be the
highest object of human ambition. It is at the bottom of all pros-
elyting and propagandism, from that of Mesmer to that of the
Church of Rome and the French Republic. That was the aposto-
late alike of Joshua and of Mahomet. Masonry alone preaches
Toleration, the right of man to abide by his own faith, the right

of all States to govern themselves. It rebukes alike the monarch who seeks to extend his dominions by conquest, the Church that claims the right to repress heresy by fire and steel, and the confederation of States that insist on maintaining a union by force and restoring brotherhood by slaughter and subjugation.

It is natural, when we are wronged, to desire revenge; and to persuade ourselves that we desire it less for our own satisfaction than to prevent a repetition of the wrong, to which the doer would be encouraged by immunity coupled with the profit of the wrong. To submit to be cheated is to encourage the cheater to continue; and we are quite apt to regard ourselves as God's chosen instruments to inflict His vengeance, and for Him and in His stead to discourage wrong by making it fruitless and its punishment sure. Revenge has been said to be "a kind of wild justice;" but it is always taken in anger, and therefore is unworthy of a great soul, which ought not to suffer its equanimity to be disturbed by ingratitude or villainy. The injuries done us by the base are as much unworthy of our angry notice as those done us by the insects and the beasts; and when we crush the adder, or slay the wolf or hyena, we should do it without being moved to anger, and with no more feeling of revenge than we have in rooting up a noxious weed.

And if it be not in human nature not to take revenge by way of punishment, let the Mason truly consider that in doing so he is God's agent, and so let his revenge be measured by justice and tempered by mercy. The law of God is, that the consequences of wrong and cruelty and crime shall be their punishment; and the injured and the wronged and the indignant are as much His instruments to enforce that law, as the diseases and public detestation, and the verdict of history and the execration of posterity are. No one will say that the Inquisitor who has racked and burned the innocent; the Spaniard who hewed Indian infants, living, into pieces with his sword, and fed the mangled limbs to his bloodhounds; the military tyrant who has shot men without trial, the knave who has robbed or betrayed his State, the fraudulent banker or bankrupt who has beggared orphans, the public officer who has violated his oath, the judge who has sold injustice, the legislator who has enabled Incapacity to work the ruin of the State, ought not to be punished. Let them be so; and let the injured or the sympathizing be the instruments of God's just vengeance; but always out of a higher feeling than mere personal revenge.

Remember that every moral characteristic of man finds its prototype among creatures of lower intelligence; that the cruel foulness of the hyena, the savage rapacity of the wolf, the merciless rage of the tiger, the crafty treachery of the panther, are found among mankind, and ought to excite no other emotion, when found in the man, than when found in the beast. Why should the true man be angry with the geese that hiss, the peacocks that strut, the asses that bray, and the apes that imitate and chatter, although they wear the human form? Always, also, it remains true, that it is more noble to forgive than to take revenge; and that, in general, we ought too much to despise those who wrong us, to feel the emotion of anger, or to desire revenge.

At the sphere of the *Sun*, you are in the region of LIGHT. * * * * The Hebrew word for *gold*, ZAHAB, also means *Light*, of which the Sun is to the Earth the great source. So, in the great Oriental allegory of the Hebrews, the River PISON compasses the land of *Gold* or *Light ;* and the River GIHON the land of *Ethiopia* or *Darkness.*

What light *is*, we no more know than the ancients did. According to the modern hypothesis, it is *not* composed of luminous particles shot out from the sun with immense velocity; but that body only impresses, on the ether which fills all space, a powerful vibratory movement that extends, in the form of luminous waves, beyond the most distant planets, supplying them with light and heat. To the ancients, it was an outflowing from the Deity. To us, as to them, it is the apt symbol of truth and knowledge. To us, also, the upward journey of the soul through the Spheres is symbolical; but we are as little informed as they whence the soul comes, where it has its origin, and whither it goes after death. They endeavored to have *some* belief and faith, *some* creed, upon those points. At the present day, men are satisfied to think nothing in regard to all that, and only to believe that the soul is a *something* separate from the body and out-living it, but whether existing before it, neither to inquire nor care. No one asks whether it emanates from the Deity, or is created out of nothing, or is generated like the body, and the issue of the souls of the father and the mother. Let us not smile, therefore, at the ideas of the ancients, until we have a better belief; but accept their symbols as meaning that the soul is of a Divine nature, originating in a sphere nearer the Deity, and returning to that when freed from the enthrallment

of the body; and that it can only return there when purified of all the sordidness and sin which have, as it were, become part of its substance, by its connection with the body.

It is not strange that, thousands of years ago, men worshipped the Sun, and that to-day that worship continues among the Parsis. Originally they looked beyond the orb to the invisible God, of whom the Sun's light, seemingly identical with generation and life, was the manifestation and outflowing. Long before the Chaldæan shepherds watched it on their plains, it came up regularly, as it now does, in the morning, like a god, and again sank, like a king retiring, in the west, to return again in due time in the same array of majesty. We worship Immutability. It was that steadfast, immutable character of the Sun that the men of Baalbec worshipped. His light-giving and life-giving powers were secondary attributes. The one grand idea that compelled worship was the characteristic of God which they saw reflected in his light, and fancied they saw in its originality the changelessness of Deity. He had seen thrones crumble, earthquakes shake the world and hurl down mountains. Beyond Olympus, beyond the Pillars of Hercules, he had gone daily to his abode, and had come daily again in the morning to behold the temples they built to his worship. They personified him as BRAHMA, AMUN, OSIRIS, BEL, ADONIS, MALKARTH, MITHRAS, and APOLLO; and the nations that did so grew old and died. Moss grew on the capitals of the great columns of his temples, and he shone on the moss. Grain by grain the dust of his temples crumbled and fell, and was borne off on the wind, and still he shone on crumbling column and architrave. The roof fell crashing on the pavement, and he shone in on the Holy of Holies with unchanging rays. It was not strange that men worshipped the Sun.

There is a water-plant, on whose broad leaves the drops of water roll about without uniting, like drops of mercury. So arguments on points of faith, in politics or religion, roll over the surface of the mind. An argument that convinces one mind has no effect on another. Few intellects, or souls that are the negations of intellect, have any logical power or capacity. There is a singular obliquity in the human mind that makes the false logic more effective than the true with nine-tenths of those who are regarded as men of intellect. Even among the judges, not one in ten can argue .ogically. Each mind sees the truth, distorted through its own

medium. Truth, to most men. is like matter in the spheroidal
state. Like a drop of cold water on the surface of a red-hot metal
plate, it dances, trembles, and spins, and never comes into contact
with it; and the mind may be plunged into truth, as the hand
moistened with sulphurous acid may into melted metal, and be not
even warmed by the immersion.

    *   *   *   *   *   *

The word *Khairûm* or *Khûrûm* is a compound one. Gesenius
renders *Khûrûm* by the word *noble* or *free-born: Khûr* meaning
white, noble. It also means the opening of a window, the socket
of the eye. *Khri* also means *white,* or an *opening ;* and *Khris,* the
orb of the Sun, in *Job,* viii. 13, and x. 7. *Krishna* is the Hindu
Sun-God. *Khur,* the Parsi word, is the literal name of the Sun.

From *Kur* or *Khur,* the Sun, comes *Khora,* a name of Lower
Egypt. The Sun, Bryant says in his Mythology, was called *Kur ;*
and Plutarch says that the Persians called the Sun *Kûros. Kurios,
Lord,* in Greek, like *Adonaï, Lord,* in Phœnician and Hebrew,
was applied to the Sun. Many places were sacred to the Sun, and
called *Kura, Kuria, Kuropolis, Kurene, Kureschata, Kuresta,* and
Corusia in Scythia.

The Egyptian Deity called by the Greeks *"Horus,"* was *Her-Ra,*
or *Har-oeris, Hor* or *Har,* the Sun. *Hari* is a Hindu name of the
Sun. *Ari-al, Ar-es, Ar, Aryaman, Areïmonios,* the AR meaning
Fire or *Flame,* are of the same kindred. *Hermes* or *Har-mês,*
(*Aram, Remus, Haram, Harameias*), was Kadmos, the Divine
Light or Wisdom. *Mar-kuri,* says Movers, is *Mar,* the Sun.

In the Hebrew, Aoor, אור, is *Light, Fire,* or the *Sun.
Cyrus,* said Ctesias, was so named from *Karos,* the Sun. *Kuris,*
Hesychius says, was Adonis. Apollo, the Sun-god, was called
Kurraios, from *Kurra,* a city in Phocis. The people of *Kurene,*
originally Ethiopians or Cutbites, worshipped the Sun under the
title of *Achoor* and *Achôr.*

We know, through a precise testimony in the ancient annals of
Tsûr, that the principal festivity of *Mal-karth,* the incarnation of
the Sun at the winter solstice, held at Tsûr, was called his *re-birth*
or his *awakening,* and that it was celebrated by means of a pyre,
on which the god was supposed to regain, through the aid of fire,
a new life. This festival was celebrated in the month *Peritius*
(*Barith*), the second day of which corresponded to the 25th of
December KHUR-UM, King of Tyre, *Movers* says, first performed

this ceremony. These facts we learn from *Josephus*, *Servius* on the *Æneid*, and the *Dionysiacs* of *Nonnus;* and through a coincidence that cannot be fortuitous, the same day was at Rome the *Dies Natalis Solis Invicti*, the festal day of the invincible Sun. Under this title, HERCULES, HAR-*acles*, was worshipped at Tsûr. Thus, while the temple was being erected, the death and resurrection of a Sun-God was annually represented at Tsûr, by Solomon's ally, at the winter solstice, by the pyre of MAL-KARTH, the Tsûrian Haracles.

AROERIS or HAR-*oeris*, the elder HORUS, is from the same old root that in the Hebrew has the form *Aûr*, or, with the definite article prefixed, *Haûr*, Light, or *the* Light, splendor, flame, the Sun and his rays. The hieroglyphic of the younger HORUS was the point in a circle; of the Elder, a pair of eyes; and the festival of the thirtieth day of the month *Epiphi*, when the sun and moon were supposed to be in the same right line with the earth, was called "*The birth-day of the eyes of Horus*."

In a papyrus published by Champollion, this god is styled "*Har oeri*, Lord of the Solar Spirits, the beneficent eye of the Sun*.*" Plutarch calls him "*Har-pocrates;*" but there is no trace of the latter part of the name in the hieroglyphic legends. He is the son of OSIRIS and ISIS; and is represented sitting on a throne supported by *lions;* the same word, in Egyptian, meaning *Lion* and *Sun*. So Solomon made a great throne of ivory, plated with gold, with six steps, at each arm of which was a lion, and one on each side to each step, making seven on each side.

Again, the Hebrew word חי, *Khi*, means "*living;*" and חאם *râm*, "*was, or shall be, raised or lifted up*." The latter is the same as רום, אום, רום, *rôom*, *arôom*, *harûm*, whence *Aram*, for Syria, or *Aramœa*, *High*-land. *Khairûm*, therefore, would mean, "*was raised up to life, or living*."

So, in Arabic, *hrm*, an unused root, meant, "*was high*," "*made great*," "*exalted*;" and *Hîrm* means an *ox*, the symbol of the Sun in Taurus, at the vernal equinox.

KHURUM, therefore, improperly called *Hiram*, is KHUR-OM, the same as *Her-ra*, *Her-mes*, and *Her-acles*, the "*Heracles Tyrius Invictus*," the personification of Light and the Son, the Mediator, Redeemer, and Saviour. From the Egyptian word *Ra* came the Coptic *Oûro*, and the Hebrew *Aûr*, Light. *Har-oeri*, is *Hor* or *Har*, the chief or *master*. *Hor* is also heat and *hora*, season or

6

hour; and hence, in several African dialects, as names of the Sun,
Airo, Ayero, eer, uiro, ghurrah, and the like. The royal name
rendered *Pharaoh,* was PHRA, that is, *Pai-ra,* the Sun.

The legend of the contest between *Hor-ra* and *Set,* or *Set-nu-bi,*
the same as *Bar* or *Bal,* is older than that of the strife between
Osiris and *Typhon;* as old, at least, as the nineteenth dynasty. It
is called in the Book of the Dead, "The day of the battle between
Horus and Set." The later myth connects itself with Phœnicia
and Syria. The body of OSIRIS went ashore at *Gebal* or *Byblos,*
sixty miles above Tsûr. You will not fail to notice that in the
name of each murderer of Khûrûm, that of the Evil God Bal is
found.

      *   *   *   *   *   *

Har-oeri was the god of TIME, as well as of Life. The Egyptian
legend was that the King of Byblos cut down the tamarisk-tree
containing the body of OSIRIS, and made of it a column for his
palace. Isis, employed in the palace, obtained possession of the
column, took the body out of it, and carried it away. Apuleius
describes her as "a beautiful female, over whose divine neck her
long thick hair hung in graceful ringlets;" and in the procession
female attendants, with ivory combs, seemed to dress and ornament
the royal hair of the goddess. The palm-tree, and the lamp in the
shape of a boat, appeared in the procession. If the symbol we are
speaking of is not a mere modern invention, it is to these things it
alludes.

The identity of the legends is also confirmed by this hieroglyphic
picture, copied from an ancient Egyptian monument, which may
also enlighten you as to the Lion's grip and the Master's gavel.

אב, in the ancient Phœnician character, 𐤀 , and in the Samaritan, 𐤀 , A B, (the two letters representing the numbers 1, 2, or Unity and Duality, means *Father*, and is a primitive noun, common to all the Semitic languages.

It also means an Ancestor, Originator, Inventor, Head, Chief or Ruler, Manager, Overseer, Master, Priest, Prophet.

אבי is simply Father, when it is in construction, that is, when it precedes another word, and in English the preposition "of" is interposed, as אבי-אל, Abi-Al, the Father of Al.

Also, the final Yôd means "my;" so that אבי by itself means "My father." דויד אבי, David my father, 2 *Chron.* ii. 2.

ו, (Vav) final is the possessive pronoun "his;" and אביו, *Abiu* (which we read "*Abif*") means "of my father's." Its full meaning, as connected with the name of Khûrûm, no doubt is, "formerly one of my father's servants," or "slaves."

The name of the Phœnician artificer is, in Samuel and Kings, חירם and חירום—[2 *Sam.* v. 11; 1 *Kings*, v. 15; 1 *Kings*, vii. 40]. In Chronicles it is חורם, with the addition of אבי. [2 *Cхron.* ii. 12]; and of אביו. [2 *Chron.* iv. 16].

It is merely absurd to add the word "*Abif*," or "*Abiff*," as part of the name of the artificer. And it is almost as absurd to add the word "*Abi*," which was a *title* and not part of the *name*. Joseph says [*Gen.* xlv. 8], "God has constituted me '*Ab l'Paraah*, as Father to Paraah, *i. e.*, Vizier or Prime Minister." So Haman was called the Second Father of Artaxerxes; and when King Khûrûm used the phrase "Khûrûm Abi," he meant that the artificer he sent Schlomoh was the principal or chief workman in his line at Tsûr.

A medal copied by Montfaucon exhibits a female nursing a child, with ears of wheat in her hand, and the legend was (Iao.) She is seated on clouds, a star at her head, and three ears of wheat rising from an altar before her.

HORUS was the *mediator*, who was buried three days, was regenerated, and triumphed over the evil principle.

The word HERI, in Sanscrit, means *Shepherd*, as well as *Saviour*. CRISHNA is called *Heri*, as JESUS called himself the *Good Shepherd*.

חור, *Khûr*, means an aperture of a window, a cave, or the eye. Also it means white. In Syriac, ܚ ܝ ܚܘܪ.

חר also means an opening, and noble, free-born, high-born.

םרח, KHRM, means consecrated, devoted; in Æthiopic ⅄ ∠◔ !
It is the name of a city, [*Josh.* xix. 38] ; and of a man, [*Ezr.* ii. 32.
x. 31; *Neh.* iii. 11].

חרה, *Khirah*, means nobility, a noble race.

Bouddha is declared to comprehend in his own person the
essence of the Hindu Trimurti; and hence the tri-literal mono-
syllable *Om* or *Aum* is applied to him as being essentially the
same as Brahma-Vishnu-Siva. He is the same as Hermes, Thoth,
Taut, and Teutates. One of his names is Heri-maya or Her-
maya, which are evidently the same name as Hermes and Khirm
or Khûrm. Heri, in Sanscrit, means *Lord.*

A learned Brother places over the two symbolic pillars, from
right to left, the two words 𐤀𐤉𐤀 and 𐤀▽𐤀 , חו and בעל, IHU
and BAL: followed by the hieroglyphic equivalent, ⌒ of the
Sun-God, Amun-ra. Is it an accidental coincidence, ⌐ 𝕝 that in
the name of each murderer are the two names of the Good and Evil
Deities of the Hebrews; for *Yu-bel* is but *Yehu-Bal* or *Yeho-Bal?*
and that the three final syllables of the names, *a, o, um,* make
A∴ U∴ M∴ the sacred word of the Hindoos, meaning the Triune-
God, Life-giving, Life-preserving, Life-destroying: represented by
the mystic character ⅄ ?

The genuine *Acacia*, also, is the thorny tamarisk, the same tree
which grew up round the body of Osiris. It was a sacred tree
among the Arabs, who made of it the idol Al-Uzza, which Mohammed destroyed. It is abundant as a bush in the Desert of
Thur: and of it the " crown of thorns" was composed, which was
set on the forehead of Jesus of Nazareth. It is a fit type of immortality on account of its tenacity of life ; for it has been known,
when planted as a door-post, to take root again and shoot out
budding boughs above the threshold.

*   *   *   *   *   *

Every commonwealth must have its periods of trial and transition, especially if it engages in war. It is certain at some time to
be wholly governed by agitators appealing to all the baser elements of the popular nature ; by moneyed corporations; by those
enriched by the depreciation of government securities or paper; by
small attorneys, schemers, money-jobbers, speculators, and adven-
turers—an ignoble oligarchy, enriched by the distresses of the State,
and fattened on the miseries of the people. Then all the deceitful
visions of equality and the rights of man end; and the wronged

and plundered State can regain a real liberty only by passing through "great varieties of untried being," purified in its transmigration by fire and blood.

In a Republic, it soon comes to pass that parties gather round the negative and positive poles of some opinion or notion, and that the intolerant spirit of a triumphant majority will allow no deviation from the standard of orthodoxy which it has set up for itself. Freedom of opinion will be professed and pretended to, but every one will exercise it at the peril of being banished from political communion with those who hold the reins and prescribe the policy to be pursued. Slavishness to party and obsequiousness to the popular whims go hand in hand. Political independence only occurs in a fossil state; and men's opinions grow out of the acts they have been constrained to do or sanction. Flattery, either of individual or people, corrupts both the receiver and the giver; and adulation is not of more service to the people than to kings. A Cæsar, securely seated in power, cares less for it than a free democracy; nor will his appetite for it grow to exorbitance, as that of a people will, until it becomes insatiate. The effect of liberty to individuals is, that they may do what they please; to a people, it is to a great extent the same. If accessible to flattery, as this is always interested, and resorted to on low and base motives, and for evil purposes, either individual or people is sure, in doing what it pleases, to do what in honor and conscience should have been left undone. One ought not even to risk congratulations, which may soon be turned into complaints; and as both individuals and peoples are prone to make a bad use of power, to flatter them, which is a sure way to mislead them, well deserves to be called a crime.

The first principle in a Republic ought to be, "that no man or set of men is entitled to exclusive or separate emoluments or privileges from the community, but in consideration of public services; which not being descendible, neither ought the offices of magistrate, legislature, or judge, to be hereditary." It is a volume of Truth and Wisdom, a lesson for the study of nations, embodied in a single sentence, and expressed in language which every man can understand. If a deluge of despotism were to overflow the world, and destroy all institutions under which freedom is protected, so that they should no longer be remembered among men, this sentence, preserved, would be suffi cient to rekindle the fires of liberty and revive the race of free men.

But, to *preserve* liberty, another must be added: "that a free State does not confer office as a reward, especially for questionable services, unless she seeks her own ruin; but all officers are *employed* by her, in consideration solely of their will and ability to render service in the future; and therefore that the best and competent are always to be preferred."

For, if there is to be any other rule, that of hereditary succession is perhaps as good as any. By no other rule is it possible to preserve the liberties of the State. By no other to intrust the power of making the laws to those only who have that keen instinctive sense of injustice and wrong which enables them to detect baseness and corruption in their most secret hiding-places, and that moral courage and generous manliness and gallant independence that make them fearless in dragging out the perpetrators to the light of day, and calling down upon them the scorn and indignation of the world. The flatterers of the people are never such men. On the contrary, a time always comes to a Republic, when it is not content, like Tiberius, with a single Sejanus, but must have a host; and when those most prominent in the lead of affairs are men without reputation, statesmanship, ability, or information, the mere hacks of party, owing their places to trickery and *want* of qualification, with none of the qualities of head or heart that make great and wise men, and, at the same time, filled with all the narrow conceptions and bitter intolerance of political bigotry. These die; and the world is none the wiser for what they have said and done. Their names sink in the bottomless pit of oblivion; but their acts of folly or knavery curse the body politic and at last prove its ruin.

Politicians, in a free State, are generally hollow, heartless, and selfish. Their own aggrandisement is the end of their patriotism; and they always look with secret satisfaction on the disappointment or fall of one whose loftier genius and superior talents overshadow their own self-importance, or whose integrity and incorruptible honor are in the way of their selfish ends. The influence of the small aspirants is always against the great man. *His* accession to power may be almost for a lifetime. One of themselves will be more easily displaced, and each hopes to succeed him; and so it at length comes to pass that men impudently

aspire to and actually win the highest stations, who are unfit for the lowest clerkships; and incapacity and mediocrity become the surest passports to office.

The consequence is, that those who feel themselves competent and qualified to serve the people, refuse with disgust to enter into the struggle for office, where the wicked and jesuitical doctrine that all is fair in politics is an excuse for every species of low villainy; and those who seek even the highest places of the State do not rely upon the power of a magnanimous spirit, on the sympathizing impulses of a great soul, to stir and move the people to generous, noble, and heroic resolves, and to wise and manly action; but, like spaniels erect on their hind legs, with fore-paws obsequiously suppliant, fawn, flatter, and actually beg for votes. Rather than descend to this, they stand contemptuously aloof, disdainfully refusing to court the people, and acting on the maxim, that "mankind has no title to demand that we shall serve them in spite of themselves."

* * * * * *

It is lamentable to see a country split into factions, each following this or that great or brazen-fronted leader with a blind, unreasoning, unquestioning hero-worship; it is contemptible to see it divided into parties, whose sole end is the spoils of victory, and their chiefs the low, the base, the venal, and the small. Such a country is in the last stages of decay, and near its end, no matter how prosperous it may seem to be. It wrangles over the volcano and the earthquake. But it is certain that no government can be conducted by the men of the people, and for the people, without a rigid adherence to those principles which our reason commends as fixed and sound. These must be the tests of parties, men, and measures. Once determined, they must be inexorable in their application, and all must either come up to the standard or declare against it. Men may betray: principles never can. Oppression is one invariable consequence of misplaced confidence in treacherous man; it is never the result of the working or application of a sound, just, well-tried principle. Compromises which bring fundamental principles into doubt, in order to unite in one party men of antagonistic creeds, are frauds, and end in ruin, the just and natural consequence of fraud. Whenever you have settled upon your theory and creed, sanction no departure from it in practice, on any ground of expediency. It is the Master's word.

Yield it up neither to flattery nor force! Let no defeat cr persecution rob you of it! Believe that he who once blundered in
statesmanship will blunder again; that such blunders are as fatal
as crimes; and that political near-sightedness does not improve
by age. There are always more impostors than seers among public
men, more false prophets than true ones, more prophets of Baal than
of Jehovah; and Jerusalem is always in danger from the Assyrians.

Sallust said that after a State has been corrupted by luxury and
idleness, it may by its mere greatness bear up under the burden of
its vices. But even while he wrote, Rome, of which he spoke, had
played out her masquerade of freedom. Other causes than luxury
and sloth destroy Republics. If small, their larger neighbors ex
tinguish them by absorption. If of great extent, the cohesive
force is too feeble to hold them together, and they fall to pieces by
their own weight. The paltry ambition of small men disintegrates
them. The want of wisdom in their councils creates exasperating
issues. Usurpation of power plays its part, incapacity seconds
corruption, the storm rises, and the fragments of the incoherent
raft strew the sandy shores, reading to mankind another lesson for
it to disregard.

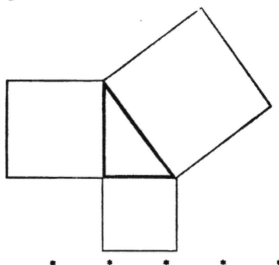

The Forty-Seventh Proposition is older than Pythagoras. It is
this: "In every right-angled triangle, the sum of the squares of the
base and perpendicular is equal to the square of the hypothennse."

The square of a number is the product of that number, multiplied by itself. Thus, 4 is the square of 2, and 9 of 3.

The first ten numbers are . 1, 2, 3,   4,   5,   6,   7,   8,   9,   10;
their squares are 1, 4, 9, 16, 25, 36, 49, 64, 81, 100;
and 3, 5,   7,   9, 11, 13, 15, 17,   19
are the differences between each square and that which precedes it; giving us the sacred numbers, 3, 5, 7, and 9.

Of these numbers, the square of 3 and 4, added together, give the square of 5; and those of 6 and 8, the square of 10; and if a right-angled triangle be formed, the base measuring 3 or 6 parts, and the perpendicular 4 or 8 parts, the hypothenuse will be 5 or 10 parts; and if a square is erected on each side, these squares being subdivided into squares each side of which is one part in length, there will be as many of these in the square erected on the hypothenuse as in the other two squares together.

Now the Egyptians arranged their deities in *Triads*,—the FATHER, or the Spirit or Active Principle or *Generative* Power; the MOTHER, or Matter, or the Passive Principle, or the *Conceptive* Power; and the SON, *Issue* or *Product*, the universe, proceeding from the two principles. These were OSIRIS, ISIS, and HORUS. In the same way, PLATO gives us *Thought*, the *Father;* Primitive *Matter* the *Mother;* and *Kosmos* the *World*, the *Son*, the universe animated by a soul. Triads of the same kind are found in the Kabalah.

PLUTARCH says, in his book *De Iside et Osiride*, "But the better and diviner nature consists of three,—that which exists within the Intellect only, and Matter, and that which proceeds from these, which the Greeks call *Kosmos;* of which three, Plato is wont to call the Intelligible, the 'Idea, Exemplar, and Father;' Matter, 'the Mother, the Nurse, and the place and receptacle of generation;' and the issue of these two, 'the Offspring and Genesis,'" the KOSMOS, "a word signifying equally *Beauty* and *Order*, or the universe itself." You will not fail to notice that Beauty is symbolized by the Junior Warden in the South. Plutarch continues to say that the Egyptians compared the universal nature to what they called the most beautiful and perfect triangle, as Plato does, in that nuptial diagram, as it is termed, which he has introduced into his Commonwealth. Then he adds that this triangle is right-angled, and its sides respectively as 3, 4, and 5; and he says, " We must suppose that the perpendicular is designed by them to represent the masculine nature, the base the feminine, and that the hypothenuse is to be looked upon as the offspring of both; and accordingly the first of them will aptly enough represent OSIRIS, or the prime cause; the second, ISIS, or the receptive capacity; the last, HORUS, or the common effect of the other two. For 3 is the first number which is composed of even and odd; and 4 is a square whose side is equal to the even number 2; but 5, being generated, as it were, out of the preceding numbers, 2 and 3, may be said to have an equal relation to both of them, as to its common parents."

    *   *   *   *   *   *

The *clasped hands* is another symbol which was used by PYTHAG-ORAS. It represented the number 10, the sacred number in which all the preceding numbers were contained; the number expressed by the mysterious TETRACTYS, a figure borrowed by him and the Hebrew priests alike from the Egyptian sacred science, and which ought to be replaced among the symbols of the Master's degree, where it of right belongs. The Hebrews formed it thus, with the letters of the Divine name:

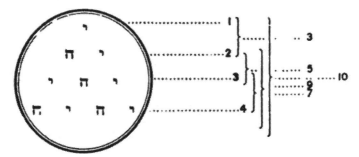

The *Tetractys* thus leads you, not only to the study of the Pythagorean philosophy as to numbers, but also to the Kabalah, and will aid you in discovering the True Word, and understanding what was meant by "The Music of the Spheres." Modern science strikingly confirms the ideas of Pythagoras in regard to the properties of numbers, and that they govern in the universe. Long before his time, nature had extracted her cube-roots and her squares.

    *   *   *   *   *   *

All the FORCES at man's disposal or under man's control, or subject to man's influence, are his *working tools*. The friendship and sympathy that knit heart to heart are a force like the attrac-

tion of cohesion, by which the sandy particles became the solid
rock. If this law of attraction or ʼnhesion were taken away, the
material worlds and suns would c..ssolve in au instant into thin
invisible vapor. If the ties of friendship, affection, and love were
annulled, mankind would become a raging multitude of wild and
savage beasts of prey. The sand hardens into rock under the immense superincumbent pressure of the ocean, aided sometimes by
the irresistible energy of fire; and when the pressure of calamity
and danger is upon an order or a country, the members or the
citizens ought to be the more closely united by the cohesion of
sympathy and inter-dependence.

Morality is a force. It is the magnetic attraction of the heart
toward Truth and Virtue. The needle, imbued with this mystic
property, and pointing unerringly to the north, carries the mariner safely over the trackless ocean, through storm and darkness,
until his glad eyes behold the beneficent beacons that welcome him
to safe and hospitable harbor. Then the hearts of those that love
him are gladdened, and his home made happy; and this gladness
and happiness are due to the silent, unostentatious, unerring mon-
:tor that was the sailor's guide over the sweltering waters. But if
drifted too far northward, he finds the needle no longer true, but
pointing elsewhere than to the north, what a feeling of helpless-
ness falls upon the dismayed mariner, what utter loss of energy
and courage! It is as if the great axioms of morality were to fail
and be no longer true, leaving the human soul to drift helplessly,
eyeless like Prometheus, at the mercy of the uncertain, faithless
currents of the deep.

Honor and Duty are the pole-stars of a Mason, the Dioscuri, by
never losing sight of which he may avoid disastrous shipwreck.
These Palinurus watched, until, overcome by sleep, and the vessel no longer guided truly, he fell into and was swallowed up by
the insatiable sea. So the Mason who loses sight of these, and is
no longer governed by their beneficent and potential force, is
lost, and sinking out of sight, will disappear unhonored and
unwept.

The force of electricity, analogous to that of sympathy, and by
means of which great thoughts or base suggestions, the utterances
of noble or ignoble natures, flash instantaneously over the nervos
of natioɩs; the force of growth, fit type of immortality, lying
dormant three thousand years in the wheat-grains buried wiʰh

their mummies by the old Egyptians; the forces of expansion and contraction, developed in the earthquake and the tornado, and giving birth to the wonderful achievements of steam, nave their parallelisms in the moral world, in individuals, and nations. Growth is a necessity for nations as for men. Its cessation is the beginning of decay. In the nation as well as the plant it is mysterious, and it is irresistible. The earthquakes that rend nations asunder, overturn thrones, and engulf monarchies and republics, have been long prepared for, like the volcanic eruption. Revolutions have long roots in the past. The force exerted is in direct proportion to the previous restraint and compression. The true statesman ought to see in progress the causes that are in due time to produce them; and he who does not is but a blind leader of the blind.

The great changes in nations, like the geological changes of the earth, are slowly and continuously wrought. The waters, falling from Heaven as rain and dews, slowly disintegrate the granite mountains; abrade the plains, leaving hills and ridges of denudation as their monuments; scoop out the valleys, fill up the seas, narrow the rivers, and after the lapse of thousands on thousands of silent centuries, prepare the great alluvia for the growth of that plant, the snowy envelope of whose seeds is to employ the looms of the world, and the abundance or penury of whose crops shall determine whether the weavers and spinners of other realms shall have work to do or starve.

So Public Opinion is an immense force; and its currents are as inconstant and incomprehensible as those of the atmosphere. Nevertheless, in free governments, it is omnipotent; and the business of the statesman is to find the means to shape, control, and direct it. According as that is done, it is beneficial and conservative, or destructive and ruinous. The Public Opinion of the civilized world is International Law; and it is so great a force, though with no certain and fixed boundaries, that it can even constrain the victorious despot to be generous, and aid an oppressed people in its struggle for independence.

Habit is a great force; it is second nature, even in trees. It is as strong in nations as in men. So also are Prejudices, which are given to men and nations as the passions are,—as forces, valuable, if properly and skillfully availed of; destructive, if unskillfully handled.

Above all, the Love of Country, State Pride, the Love of Home, are forces of immense power. Encourage them all. Insist upon them in your public men. Permanency of home is necessary to patriotism. A migratory race will have little love of country. State pride is a mere theory and chimera, where men remove from State to State with indifference, like the Arabs, who camp here to-day and there to-morrow.

If you have Eloquence, it is a mighty force. See that you use it for good purposes—to teach, exhort, ennoble the people, and not to mislead and corrupt them. Corrupt and venal orators are the assassins of the public liberties and of public morals.

The Will is a force; its limits as yet unknown. It is in the power of the will that we chiefly see the spiritual and divine in man. There is a seeming identity between his will that moves other men, and the Creative Will whose action seems so incomprehensible. It is the men of *will* and *action*, not the men of pure intellect, that govern the world.

Finally, the three greatest moral forces are FAITH, which is the only true WISDOM, and the very foundation of all government; HOPE, which is STRENGTH, and insures success; and CHARITY, which is BEAUTY, and alone makes animated, united effort possible. These forces are within the reach of all men; and an association of men, actuated by them, ought to exercise an immense power in the world. If Masonry does not, it is because she has ceased to possess them.

Wisdom in the man or statesman, in king or priest, largely consists in the due appreciation of these forces; and upon the general *non*-appreciation of some of them the fate of nations often depends. What hecatombs of lives often hang upon the not weighing or not sufficiently weighing the force of an idea, such as, for example, the reverence for a flag, or the blind attachment to a form or constitution of government!

What errors in political economy and statesmanship are committed in consequence of the over-estimation or under-estimation of particular values, or the non-estimation of some among them! Everything, it is asserted, is the product of human labor; but the gold or the diamond which one accidentally finds without labor is not so. What is the value of the labor bestowed by the husbandman upon his crops, compared with the value of the sunshine and rain, without which his labor avails nothing? Commerce carried on by the labor of man, adds to the value of the products of the field, the mine, or the workshop, by their transportation tc different markets; but how much of this increase is due to the rivers down which these products float, to the winds that urge the keels of commerce over the ocean!

Who can estimate the value of morality and manliness in a State, of moral worth and intellectual knowledge? These are the sunshine and rain of the State. The winds, with their changeable, fickle, fluctuating currents, are apt emblems of the fickle humors of the populace, its passions, its heroic impulses, its enthusiasms. Woe to the statesman who does not estimate these as values!

Even music and song are sometimes found to have an incalculable value. Every nation has some song of a proven value, more easily counted in lives than dollars. The Marseillaise was worth to revolutionary France, who shall say how many thousand men?

Peace also is a great element of prosperity and wealth; a value not to be calculated. Social intercourse and association of men in beneficent Orders have a value not to be estimated in coin. The illustrious examples of the Past of a nation, the memories and immortal thoughts of her great and wise thinkers, statesmen, and heroes, are the invaluable legacy of that Past to the Present and future. And all these have not only the values of the loftier and more excellent and priceless kind, but also an actual *money*-value, since it is only when co-operating with or aided or enabled by these, that human labor creates wealth. They are of the chief elements of material wealth, as they are of national manliness, heroism, glory, prosperity, and immortal renown.

* * * * * *

Providence has appointed the three great disciplines of *War*, the *Monarchy* and the *Priesthood*, all that the CAMP, the PALACE, and the TEMPLE may symbolize, to train the multitudes forward to intelligent and premeditated combinations for all the great purposes of society. The result will at length be free governments among men, when virtue and intelligence become qualities of the multitudes; but for ignorance such governments are impossible. Man advances only by degrees. The removal of one pressing calamity gives courage to attempt the removal of the remaining evils, rendering men more sensitive to them, or perhaps sensitive for the first time. Serfs that writhe under the whip are not disquieted about their political rights; manumitted from personal slavery, they bo come sensitive to political oppression. Liberated from arbitrary power, and governed by the law alone, they begin to scrutinize the law itself, and desire to be governed, not only by law, but oy what they deem the best law. And when the civil or temporal despot ism has been set aside, and the municipal law has been moulded on the principles of an enlightened jurisprudence, they may wake to the discovery that they are living under some priestly or ecclesiastical despotism, and become desirous of working a reformation there also.

It is quite true that the advance of humanity is slow, and that it often pauses and retrogrades. In the kingdoms of the earth we do not see despotisms retiring and yielding the ground to self-governing communities. We do not see the churches and priesthoods of Christendom relinquishing their old task of governing men by imaginary terrors. Nowhere do we see a populace that could be safely manumitted from such a government. We do not see the great religious teachers aiming to discover truth for themselves and for others; but still ruling the world, and contented and compelled to rule the world, by whatever dogma is already accredited; themselves as much bound down by this necessity to govern, as the populace by their need of government. Poverty in all its most hideous forms still exists in the great cities; and the cancer of pauperism has its roots in the hearts of kingdoms. Men there take no measure of their wants and their own power to supply them, but live and multiply like the beasts of the field,—Providence having apparently ceased to care for them. Intelligence never visits these, or it makes its appearance as some new development of villainy. War has not ceased; still there are battles and sieges. Homes are still unhappy, and tears and anger and spite make hells where there should be heavens. So much the more necessity for Masonry! So much wider the field of its labors! So much the more need for it to begin to be true to itself, to revive from its asphyxia, to repent of its apostacy to its true creed!

Undoubtedly, labor and death and the sexual passion are essential and permanent conditions of human existence, and render perfection and a millenium on earth impossible. Always,—it is the decree of Fate!—the vast majority of men must toil to live, and cannot find time to cultivate the intelligence. Man, knowing he is to die, will not sacrifice the present enjoyment for a greater one in the future. The love of woman cannot die out; and it has a

terrible and uncontrollable fate, increased by the refinements of
civilization. Woman is the veritable syren or goddess of the
young. But society can be improved; and free government is
possible for States; and freedom of thought and conscience is no
longer *wholly* utopian. Already we see that Emperors prefer to be
elected by universal suffrage; that States are conveyed to Empires
by vote; and that Empires are administered with something of the
spirit of a Republic, being little else than democracies with a single
head, ruling through one man, one representative, instead of an
assembly of representatives. And if Priesthoods still govern, they
now come before the laity to prove, by stress of argument, that they
ought to govern. They are obliged to evoke the very reason which
they are bent on supplanting.

Accordingly, men become daily more free, because the freedom
of the man lies in his reason. He can reflect upon his own future
conduct, and summon up its consequences; he can take wide views
of human life, and lay down rules for constant guidance. Thus
he is relieved of the tyranny of sense and passion, and enabled at
any time to live according to the whole light of the knowledge
that is within him, instead of being driven, like a dry leaf on the
wings of the wind, by every present impulse. Herein lies the freedom of the man as regarded in connection with the necessity imposed by the omnipotence and fore-knowledge of God. So much
light, so much liberty. When emperor and church appeal to reason there is naturally universal suffrage.

Therefore no one need lose courage, nor believe that labor in the
cause of Progress will be labor wasted. There is no waste in nature, either of Matter, Force, Act, or Thought. A Thought is as
much the end of life as an Action; and a single Thought sometimes
works greater results than a Revolution, even Revolutions themselves. Still there should not be divorce between Thought and
Action. The true Thought is that in which life culminates. But
all wise and true Thought produces Action. It is generative, like
the light; and light and the deep shadow of the passing cloud are
the gifts of the prophets of the race. Knowledge, laboriously
acquired, and inducing habits of sound Thought,—the reflective
character,—must necessarily be rare. The multitude of laborers
cannot acquire it. Most men attain to a very low standard of it.
It is incompatible with the ordinary and indispensable avocations
of life. A whole world of error as well as of labor, go to make

one reflective man. In the most advanced nation of Europe there are more ignorant than wise, more poor than rich, more automatic laborers, the mere creatures of habit, than reasoning and reflective men. The proportion is at least a thousand to one. Unanimity of opinion is so obtained. It only exists among the multitude who do not think, and the political or spiritual priesthood who think for that multitude, who think how to guide and govern them. When men begin to reflect, they begin to differ. The great problem is to find guides who will not seek to be tyrants. This is needed even more in respect to the heart than the head. Now, every man earns his special share of the produce of human labor, by an incessant scramble, by trickery and deceit. Useful knowledge, honorably acquired, is too often used after a fashion not honest or reasonable, so that the studies of youth are far more noble than the practices of manhood. The labor of the farmer in his fields, the generous returns of the earth, the benignant and favoring skies, tend to make him earnest, provident, and grateful; the education of the market-place makes him querulous, crafty, envious, and an intolerable niggard.

Masonry seeks to be this beneficent, unambitious, disinterested guide; and it is the very condition of all great structures that the sound of the hammer and the clink of the trowel should be always heard in some part of the building. With faith in man, hope for the future of humanity, loving-kindness for our fellows, Masonry and the Mason must always work and teach. Let each do that for which he is best fitted. The teacher also is a workman. Praiseworthy as the active navigator is, who comes and goes and makes one clime partake of the treasures of the other, and one to share the treasures of all, he who keeps the beacon-light upon the hill is also at his post.

Masonry has already helped cast down some idols from their pedestals, and grind to impalpable dust some of the links of the chains that held men's souls in bondage. That there has been progress needs no other demonstration than that you may now reason with men, and urge upon them, without danger of the rack or stake, that no doctrines can be apprehended as truths if they contradict each other, or contradict other truths given us by God. Long before the Reformation, a monk, who had found his way to heresy without the help of Martin Luther, not venturing to breathe alord into any living ear his anti-papal and trea-

7

sonable doctrines, wrote them on parchment, and sealing t p the
perilous record, hid it in the massive walls of his monastery.
There was no friend or brother to whom he could intrust his
secret or pour forth his soul. It was some consolation to imagine
that in a future age some one might find the parchment, and the
seed be found not to have been sowed in vain. What if the truth
should have to lie dormant as long before germinating as the wheat
in the Egyptian mummy? Speak it, nevertheless, again and
again, and let it take its chance!

The rose of Jericho grows in the sandy deserts of Arabia and
on the Syrian housetops. Scarcely six inches high, it loses its
leaves after the flowering season, and dries up into the form of a
ball. Then it is uprooted by the winds, and carried, blown, or
tossed across the desert, into the sea. There, feeling the contact
of the water, it unfolds itself, expands its branches, and expels its
seeds from their seed-vessels. These, when saturated with water,
are carried by the tide and laid on the sea-shore. Many are lost,
as many individual lives of men are useless. But many are
thrown back again from the sea-shore into the desert, where, by
the virtue of the sea-water that they have imbibed, the roots and
leaves sprout and they grow into fruitful plants, which will, in
their turns, like their ancestors, be whirled into the sea. God will
not be less careful to provide for the germination of the truths
you may boldly utter forth. "*Cast*," He has said, "*thy bread upon
the waters, and after many days it shall return to thee again.*"

Initiation does not change: we find it again and again, and
always the same, through all the ages. The last disciples of Pas-
calis Martinez are still the children of Orpheus; but they adore
the realizer of the antique philosophy, the Incarnate Word of the
Christians.

Pythagoras, the great divulger of the philosophy of numbers,
visited all the sanctuaries of the world. He went into Judæa,
where he procured himself to be circumcised, that he might be
admitted to the secrets of the Kabalah, which the prophets Ezekiel
and Daniel, not without some reservations, communicated to him.
Then, not without some difficulty, he succeeded in being admitted
to the Egyptian initiation, upon the recommendation of King
Amasis. The power of his genius supplied the deficiencies or the
imperfect communications of the Hierophants, and he himself
became a Master and a Revealer.

Pythagoras defined God: a Living and Absolute Verity clothed with Light.

He said that the Word was Number manifested by Form.

He made all descend from the *Tetractys*, that is to say, from the Quaternary.

God, he said again, is the Supreme Music, the nature of which is Harmony.

Pythagoras gave the magistrates of Crotona this great religious, political, and social precept:

"There is no evil that is not preferable to Anarchy."

Pythagoras said, "Even as there are three divine notions and three intelligible regions, so there is a triple word, for the Hierarchical Order always manifests itself by threes. There are the word simple, the word hieroglyphical, and the word symbolic: in other terms, there are the word that expresses, the word that conceals, and the word that signifies; the whole hieratic intelligence is in the perfect knowledge of these three degrees."

Pythagoras enveloped doctrine with symbols, but carefully eschewed personifications and images, which, he thought, sooner or later produced idolatry.

The Holy Kabalah, or tradition of the children of Seth, was carried from Chaldæa by Abraham, taught to the Egyptian priesthood by Joseph, recovered and purified by Moses, concealed under symbols in the Bible, revealed by the Saviour to Saint John, and contained, entire, under hieratic figures analogous to those of all antiquity, in the Apocalypse of that Apostle.

The Kabalists consider God as the Intelligent, Animating, Living Infinite. He is not, for them, either the aggregate of existences, or existence in the abstract, or a being philosophically definable. He is *in* all, *distinct* from all, and *greater* than all. His name even is ineffable; and yet this name only expresses the human ideal of His divinity. What God is in Himself, it is not given to man to comprehend.

God is the absolute of Faith; but the absolute of *Reason* is BEING, יהוה. "*I am that I am*," is a wretched translation.

Being, Existence, is by itself, and because it Is. The reason of Being, is Being itself. We may inquire, "Why does something exist?" that is, "Why does such or such a thing exist?" But we cannot, without being absurd, ask, "Why Is Being?" That would be to suppose Being before Being. If Being had a

cause, that cause would necessarily Be; that is, the cause and
effect would be identical.

Reason and science demonstrate to us that the modes of Existence and Being balance each other in equilibrium according to
harmonious and hierarchic laws. But a hierarchy is synthetized.
in ascending, and becomes ever more and more monarchical. Yet
the reason cannot pause at a single chief, without being alarmed
at the abysses which it seems to leave above this Supreme Monarch. Therefore it is silent, and gives place to the Faith it adores.

What is certain, even for science and the reason, is, that the
idea of God is the grandest, the most holy, and the most useful of
all the aspirations of man; that upon this belief morality reposes,
with its eternal sanction. This belief, then, is in humanity, the
most real of the phenomena of being; and if it were false, nature
would affirm the absurd; nothingness would give form to life, and
God would at the same time be and not be.

It is to this philosophic and incontestable reality, which is
termed The Idea of God, that the Kabalists give a name. In
this name all others are contained. Its cyphers contain all the
numbers; and the hieroglyphics of its letters express all the laws
and all the things of nature.

BEING IS BEING: the reason of Being is in Being: in the Beginning is the Word, and the Word in logic formulated Speech,
the spoken Reason; the Word is in God, and is God Himself, manifested to the Intelligence. Here is what is above all the philoso-
phies. This we must believe, under the penalty of never truly
knowing anything, and relapsing into the absurd skepticism of
Pyrrho. The Priesthood, custodian of Faith, wholly rests upon
this basis of knowledge, and it is in its teaching we must recognize the Divine Principle of the Eternal Word.

Light is not Spirit, as the Indian Hierophants believed it to be;
but only the instrument of the Spirit. It is not the body of the
Protoplastes, as the Theurgists of the school of Alexandria taught,
but the first physical manifestation of the Divine afflatus. God
eternally creates it, and man, in the image of God, modifies and
seems to multiply it.

The high magic is styled "The Sacerdotal Art," and "The
Royal Art." In Egypt, Greece, and Rome, it could not but share
the greatnesses and decadences of the Priesthood and of Royalty.
Every philosophy hostile to the national worship and to its myste

nes, was of necessity hostile to the great political powers, which lose their grandeur, if they cease, in the eyes of the multitudes, to be the images of the Divine Power. Every Crown is shattered, when it clashes against the Tiara.

Plato, writing to Dionysius the Younger, in regard to the natuie of the First Principle, says: "I must write to you in enigmas, so that if my letter be intercepted by land or sea, he who shall read it may in no degree comprehend it." And then he says, "All things surround their King; they are, on account of Him, and He alone is the cause of good things, Second for the Seconds and Third for the Thirds."

There is in these few words a complete summary of the Theology of the Sephiroth. "The *King*" is AINSOPH, Being Supreme and Absolute. From this centre, *which is everywhere*, all things ray forth ; but we especially conceive of it in three manners and in three different spheres. In the *Divine* world (AZILUTH), which is that of the First Cause, and wherein the whole Eternity of Things in the beginning existed as Unity, to be afterward, during Eternity uttered forth, clothed with form, and the attributes that constitute them matter, the First Principle is Single and First, and yet not the VERY Illimitable Deity, incomprehensible, undefinable; but Himself in so far as manifested by the Creative Thought. To compare littleness with infinity,—Arkwright, as inventor of the spinning-jenny, and not the *man* Arkwright *otherwise* and *beyond that*. All we can know of the Very God is, compared to His Wholeness, only as an infinitesimal fraction of a unit, compared with an infinity of Units.

In the World of Creation, which is that of Second Causes [the Kabalistic World BRIAH], the Autocracy of the First Principle is complete, but we conceive of it only as the Cause of the Second Causes. Here it is manifested by the Binary, and is the Creative Principle passive. Finally: in the third world, YEZIRAH, or of Formation, it is revealed in the perfect Form, the Form of Forms, the Word, the Supreme Beauty and Excellence, the Created Perfection. Thus the Principle is at once the First, the Second, and the Third, since it is All in All, the Centre and Cause of all. It is not *the genius of Plato* that we here admire. We recognize only *the exact knowledge of the Initiate.*

The great Apostle Saint John did not borrow from the philosophy of Plato the opening of his Gospel. Plato, on the contrary drank at the same springs with Saint John and Philo; and John in the opening verses of his paraphrase, states the first principles of a dogma common to many schools, but in language especially belonging to Philo, whom it is evident he had read. The philosophy of Plato, the greatest of human Revealers, could *yearn toward* the Word made man; the Gospel alone could give him to the world.

Doubt, in presence of Being and its harmonies; skepticism, in the face of the eternal mathematics and the immutable laws of Life which make the Divinity present and visible everywhere, as the Human is known and visible by its utterances of word and act,—is this not the most foolish of superstitions, and the most inexcusable as well as the most dangerous of all credulities? Thought, we know, is not a result or consequence of the organization of matter, of the chemical or other action or reaction of its particles, like effervescence and gaseous explosions. On the contrary, the fact that Thought is manifested and realized in act human or act divine, proves the existence of an Entity, or Unity, that thinks. And the Universe is the Infinite Utterance of one of an infinite number of Infinite Thoughts, which cannot but emanate from an Infinite and Thinking Source. The cause is always equal, at least, to the effect; and matter cannot think, nor could it cause itself, or exist without cause, nor could nothing *produce* either forces or things; for in void nothingness no Forces can inhere. Admit a self-existent Force, and its Intelligence, or an Intelligent cause of it, is admitted, and at once GOD IS.

The Hebrew allegory of the Fall of Man, which is but a special variation of a universal legend, symbolizes one of the grandest and most universal allegories of science.

Moral Evil is Falsehood in actions; as Falsehood is Crime in words

Injustice is the essence of Falsehood; and every false word is an injustice.

Injustice is the death of the Moral Being, as Falsehood is the poison of the Intelligence.

The perception of the Light is the dawn of the Eternal Life, in Being. The Word of God, which creates the Light, seems to be uttered by every Intelligence that can take cognizance of Forms and will look. "Let the Light BE! The Light, in fact, exists, in its condition of splendor, for those eyes alone that gaze at it; and the Soul, amorous of the spectacle of the beauties of the universe, and applying its attention to that luminous writing of the Infinite Book, which is called "The Visible," seems to utter, as God did on the dawn of the first day, that sublime and creative word, "BE! LIGHT!"

It is not beyond the tomb, but in life itself, that we are to seek for the mysteries of death. Salvation or reprobation begins here below, and the terrestrial world too has its Heaven and its Hell. Always, even here below, virtue is rewarded; always, even here below, vice is punished; and that which makes us sometimes believe in the impunity of evil-doers is that riches, those instruments of good and of evil, seem sometimes to be given them at hazard. But woe to unjust men, when they possess the key of gold! It opens, for *them*, only the gate of the tomb and of Hell.

All the true Initiates have recognized the usefulness of toil and sorrow. "Sorrow," says a German poet, "is the dog of that unknown shepherd who guides the flock of men." To learn to suffer, to learn to die, is the discipline of Eternity, the immortal Noviciate.

The allegorical picture of Cebes, in which the Divine Comedy of Dante was sketched in Plato's time, the description whereof has been preserved for us, and which many painters of the middle age have reproduced by this description, is a monument at once philosophical and magical. It is a most complete moral synthesis, and at the same time the most audacious demonstration ever given of the Grand Arcanum, of that secret whose revelation would overturn Earth and Heaven. Let no one expect us to give them its explanation! He who passes behind the veil that hides this mystery, understands that it is in its very nature inexplicable, and that it is death to those who win it by surprise, as well as to him who reveals it.

This secret is the Royalty of the Sages, the Crown of the Initiate whom we see redescend victorious from the summit of Trials, in the fine allegory of Cebes. The Grand Arcanum makes him master of gold and the light, which are at bottom the same thing, he has solved the problem of the quadrature of the circle, he directs the perpetual movement, and he possesses the philosophical stone. Here the Adepts will understand us. There is neither interruption in the toil of nature, nor gap in her work. The Harmonies of Heaven correspond to those of Earth, and the Eternal Life accomplishes its evolutions in accordance with the same laws as the life of a dog. "God has arranged all things by weigh.; number, and measure," says the Bible; and this luminous doctrine was also that of Plato.

Humanity has never really had but one religion and one worship. This universal light has had its uncertain mirages, its deceitful reflections, and its shadows; but always, after the nights of Error, we see it reappear, one and pure like the Sun.

The magnificences of worship are the life of religion, and if Christ wishes poor ministers, His Sovereign Divinity does not wish paltry altars. Some Protestants have not comprehended that worship is a teaching, and that we must not create in the imagination of the multitude a mean or miserable God. Those oratories that resemble poorly-furnished offices or inns, and those worthy ministers clad like notaries or lawyers' clerks, do they not necessarily cause religion to be regarded as a mere puritanic formality, and God as a Justice of the Peace.

We scoff at the Augurs. It is so easy to scoff, and so difficult well to comprehend. Did the Deity leave the whole world without Light for two score centuries, to illuminate only a little corner of Palestine and a brutal, ignorant, and ungrateful people? Why always calumniate God and the Sanctuary? Were there never any others than rogues among the priests? Could no honest and sincere men be found among the Hierophants of Ceres or Diana, of Dionusos or Apollo, of Hermes or Mithras? Were these, then, all deceived, like the rest? Who, then, constantly deceived them, without betraying themselves, during a series of centuries?—for the cheats are not immortal! Arago said, that outside of the pure mathematics, he who utters the word "impossible," is wanting in prudence and good sense.

The true name of Satan, the Kabalists say, is that of Yahveh reversed; for Satan is not a black god, but the negation of God. The Devil is the personification of Atheism or Idolatry.

For the Initiates, this is not a *Person*, but a *Force*, created for good, but which *may* serve for evil. *It is the instrument of Liberty or Free Will.* They represent this Force, which presides over the physical generation, under the mythologic and horned form of the God PAN; thence came the he-goat of the Sabbat, brother of the Ancient Serpent, and the Light-bearer or *Phosphor*, of which the poets have made the false Lucifer of the legend.

Gold, to the eyes of the Initiates, is Light condensed.

They restyle the sacred numbers of the Kabalah "golden numbers," and the moral teachings of Pythagoras his "golden verses." For the same reason, a mysterious book of Apuleus in which an ass figures largely, was called "The Golden Ass."

The Pagans accused the Christians of worshipping an ass, and they did not invent this reproach, but it came from the Samaritan Jews, who, figuring the data of the Kabalah in regard to the Divinity by Egyptian symbols, also represented the Intelligence by the figure of the Magical Star adored under the name of *Remphan*, Science under the emblem of Anubis, whose name they changed to *Nibbas*, and the vulgar faith or credulity under the figure of *Thartac*, a god represented with a book, a cloak, and the head of an ass. According to the Samaritan Doctors, Christianity was the reign of *Thartac*, blind Faith and vulgar credulity erected into a universal oracle, and preferred to Intelligence and Science.

Synesius, Bishop of Ptolemais, a great Kabalist, but of doubtful orthodoxy, wrote:

"The people will always mock at things easy to be understood; it must needs have impostures."

"A Spirit," he said, "that loves wisdom and contemplates the Truth close at hand, is forced to disguise it, to induce the multitudes to accept it. . . . . Fictions are necessary to the people, and the Truth becomes deadly to those who are not strong enough to contemplate it in all its brilliance. If the sacerdotal laws allowed the reservation of judgments and the allegory of words, I would accept the proposed dignity on condition that I might be a philosopher at home, and abroad a narrator of apologues and parables. . . . In fact, what can there be in common between the vile multitude and sublime wisdom ? The truth must be kept secret, and the masses need a teaching proportioned to their imperfect reason."

Moral disorders produce physical ugliness, and in some sort realize those frightful faces which tradition assigns to the demons.

The first Druids were the true children of the Magi, and their initiation came from Egypt and Chaldæa, that is to say, from the pure sources of the primitive Kabalah. They adored the Trinity under the names of *Isis* or *Ilesus*, the Supreme Harmony; of *Belen* or *Bel*, which in Assyrian means Lord, a name correspond-ing to that of ADONAI; and of *Camul* or *Camaël*, a name that in the Kabalah personifies the Divine Justice. Below this triangle of light they supposed a divine reflection, also composed of three per sonified rays; first, *Teutates* or *Teuth,* the same as the *Thot* of the Egyptians, the Word, or the Intelligence formulated ; then Force and Beauty, whose names varied like their emblems. Finally, they completed the sacred Septenary by a mysterious Image that represented the progress of the dogma and its future realizations. This was a young girl veiled, holding a child in her arms; and they dedicated this image to "The Virgin who will become a mother;— *Virgini parituros."*

Hertha or Wertha, the young Isis of Gaul, Queen of Heaven, the Virgin who was to bear a child, held the spindle of the Fates, filled with wool half white and half black ; because she presides over all forms and all symbols, and weaves the garment of the Ideas.

One of the most mysterious pantacles of the Kabalah, contained in the Enchiridion of Leo III., represents an equilateral triangle reversed, inscribed in a double circle. On the triangle are writ-ten, in such manner as to form the prophetic Tau, the two Hebrew words so often found appended to the Ineffable Name, אלהים and צבאות, ALOHAYIM, or the Powers, and TSABAOTH, or the Starry Armies and their guiding spirits; words also which symbolize the Equilibrium of the Forces of Nature and the Harmony of Num-bers. To the three sides of the triangle belong the three great Names יהוה, אדני, and אגלא, IAHAVEH,. ADONAÏ, and AGLA. Above the first is written in Latin, *Formatio,* above the second *Reformatio,* and above the third, *Transformatio.* So Creation is ascribed to the FATHER, Redemption or Reformation to the SON, and Sanctification or Transformation to the HOLY SPIRIT, answer· ing unto the mathematical laws of Action, Reaction, and Equilib- rium. IAHAVEH is also, in effect, the Genesis or Formation of dogma, by the elementary signification of the four letters of the Sacred Tetragram ; ADON AÏ is the realization of this dogma in the Human Form, in the Visible LORD, who is the Son of God or the perfect Man; and AGLA (formed of the initials of the four words Ath Gebur laulaim Adonai) expresses the synthesis of the whole dogma and the totality of the Kabalistic science, clearly indicat- ing by the hieroglyphics of which this admirable name is formed the Triple Secret of the Great Work.

Masonry, like all the Religions, all the Mysteries, Hermeticism and Alchemy, *conceals* its secrets from all except the Adepts and Sages, or the Elect, and uses false explanations and misinterpretations of its symbols to mislead those who deserve only to be mis led; to conceal the Truth, which it calls Light, from them, and to draw them away from it. Truth is not for those who are unworthy or unable to receive it, or would pervert it. So God Himself incapacitates many men, by color-blindness, to distinguish colors, and leads the masses away from the highest Truth, giving them the power to attain only so much of it as it is profitable to them to know. Every age has had a religion suited to its capacity.

The Teachers, even of Christianity, are, in general, the most ignorant of the true meaning of that which they teach. There is no book of which so little is known as the Bible. To most who read it, it is as incomprehensible as the Sohar.

So Masonry jealously conceals its secrets, and intentionally leads conceited interpreters astray. There is no sight under the sun more pitiful and ludicrous at once, than the spectacle of the Prestons and the Webbs, not to mention the later incarnations of Dullness and Commonplace, undertaking to "explain" the old symbols of Masonry, and adding to and "improving" them, or inventing new ones.

To the Circle inclosing the central point, and itself traced between two parallel lines, a figure purely Kabalistic, these persons have added the superimposed Bible, and even reared on that the ladder with three or nine rounds, and then given a vapid interpretation of the whole, so profoundly absurd as actually to escute admiration.

Printed in Poland
by Amazon Fulfillment
Poland Sp. z o.o., Wrocław

30264497R00079